40 d Heather

Indian Summer

Copyright © 1981 by
April Swayne-Thomas

First published in Great Britain
by New English Library Limited,
Barnard's Inn, Holborn,
London EC1N 2JR in 1981

All rights reserved. No part of
this publication may be
reproduced or transmitted in
any form or by any means,
without permission of the
publishers.

Designed by Ian Hughes
Photography by Alan Philip
Set in 12pt Times by
Modern Text Typesetting
Printed and bound in Hong Kong
by Mandarin Publishers Ltd.

ISBN: 0 450 04850 0

All of the illustrations in this book, some of them studies for larger works such as murals, are taken from the drawings made by the author during the periods covered by the letters that form the text. Some drawings are not directly related to the text but are included because they beautifully capture the Indian sub-continent so keenly observed and loved by the author.

Indian Summer
A Mem-sahib in India and Sind

April Swayne-Thomas

with illustrations from the author's drawings
and a Foreword by
Sir Sidney Ridley, ICS

NEW ENGLISH LIBRARY
TIMES MIRROR

For Geoffrey
and all those who can remember

April Swayne-Thomas; portrait by M. I. E. Pullan, Gold Medallist, Paris Salon, 1972.

Foreword
By Sir Sydney Ridley, I.C.S.

I feel honoured to be invited to write the Foreword to this book, which I am sure will make an immediate appeal to readers. The art of letter-writing is one which is slowly losing the battle for survival, due to progress in the development of communications, the telephone, T.V. screen, etc. which make letter-writing almost redundant.

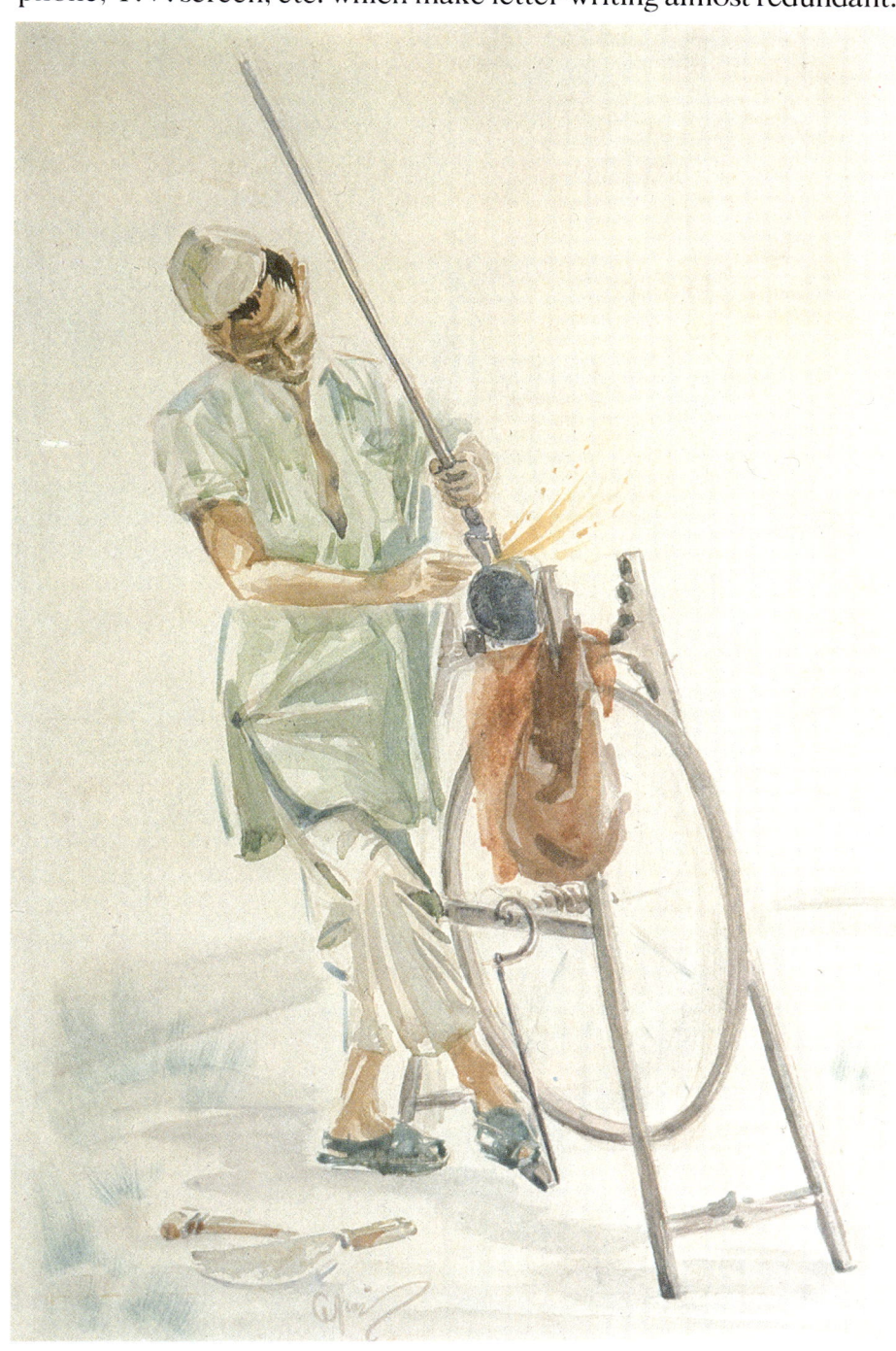

Sindi knife-grinder.

But these new skills cannot diminish the pleasure of reading letters of earlier times.

The letters in this book cover two periods, 1940 to 1947 and 1952 to 1954–years of tremendous importance in the history of the Indian sub-continent. After Partition, in 1947, there was in Britain an understandable lack of interest in the affairs of the sub-continent, as this presaged the break-up of the Empire. But now that the process of break-up has almost run its course, interest in the history of the sub-continent has been rekindled. And though the letters in this book deal mainly with matters remote from the great military and political events of the period, it is as well to keep those events in the mind as a background.

The pre-Partition period covered by the first batch of letters is particularly important and interesting. The letters commence in the early part of the Second World War, which found Geoffrey and April in Karachi, Geoffrey being in the Royal Engineers. I was District Magistrate at the time. In 1942, Congress launched its Civil Disobedience Campaign. Most of the Congress leaders were held in detention. There were meetings and demonstrations in the streets in defiance of prohibitory orders, but these were dispersed by Police using light canes. Karachi was probably the only city of its size in India to come through those years of unrest without a single shot being fired by the Police in the maintenance of order. So the general political atmosphere in Sind was much less disturbed than elsewhere in India. At the same time, the Germans were making startling advances on the Eastern Front, and at one time it seemed likely that they would break through the Caucasus and so threaten India. Stalingrad saved the situation. On the eastern border, also, there was grave danger from the Japanese, who had occupied Burma. Then came the Allied victories in North Africa and Italy, the landings in France, the fall of Germany and, a few months later, of Japan. Momentous days. There followed nearly two years of sparring between Congress and the Muslim League and, finally, the decision to partition the country.

When the war ended, Geoffrey was given assignments which meant extensive travelling throughout India; of this, April took the fullest advantage and the results are mirrored in this book.

The second set of letters have a quieter and more peaceful background. Geoffrey had already produced a report for the Government of Sind, recommending the manner in which the City of Karachi should be developed, as the population was now increasing rapidly. He and April then migrated to Australia, where they spent three years, Geoffrey again being employed in town-planning in Canberra. In the meantime, the Government of Pakistan had by enactment taken over from the Government of Sind control of Karachi and its immediate environs, so that Sind no longer had a capital. The Sind Government, therefore, on my recommendation, invited Geoffrey to plan a new Provincial capital. He readily agreed and so returned to Sind, and it was during the two years he spent working out his plans for Hyderabad as the capital City that the

On the Brahmaputra.

letters were written by April. By this time, the mass movement of refugees was over; Hindus had abandoned all the major cities and towns in Sind, and the property they had abandoned was allotted to refugees. But refugees had still to be housed and maintained in camps until more permanent settlements could be arranged. Administrative problems were infinite, and everyone in some way or other was affected by the refugee problem.

Against this sombre background, it is most refreshing to read April's letters describing the places she visited, the people she met, the scenes she witnessed and the gems of conversation she heard. The letters reveal her own natural reaction to events, with no intention merely to please. Herself an artist of standing, she saw detail which the ordinary person would have missed. And her descriptions are naturally picturesque; they are literally paintings in words. She was obviously greatly helped by Geoffrey's sense of humour.

Facing page:
Mural in the author's home.

Prominent throughout the letters is their love of animals and their preparedness to do anything to alleviate suffering; it was just part of their lives. It is almost axiomatic that in any country where the greater part of the population lives on or below the poverty line, cruelty to animals should be common practice. Why worry about animals when so many human beings around you are suffering daily from want? But Geoffrey and April felt they had a mission and they carried it out as far as possible wherever they went.

To people living in those times who received the letters, they must have proved a refreshing tonic. Those who read them now, and are able to see some of April's exquisite drawings that appear in these pages, will get a very colourful picture of life as it really was in the old India and the early years of Pakistan.

S.R.
Bridport, Dorset
August, 1980

Fishing on the Brahmaputra.

Part One

1940 to 1947

Karachi in August

We have had RAIN — that may mean nothing much to you but here in Sind the rains come once a year, if at all, and for the past three years we have had an inch or two in a week per YEAR, (suits me, after Lancs.) but this year there has been an utter DELUGE that was only equalled in 1893 — homes and people and cattle have been swept away, rivers, which for years have just been a rather large desert road with a railway bridge over them and one wondered what for, have become raging torrents overnight. Not a house in this town is built to stand RAIN on the roofs, or roads; the little we ever have is not worth the expense of proper tiles, gutters and drainage so that all roads are lakes and if you live in a flat you may not have even *one* dry spot in it. Here in our bungalow of lots of rooms and big verandas we have been able to camp out and have stranded Air Force billeted on us and house two families of servants whose little house in the compound has just fallen down! My clothes are *green* in the wardrobe overnight and we have a LAWN again.

Karachi, Sind
November 1941

They say that this card will reach you on Christmas Day, and bring my greetings and love with it. It is difficult to imagine November at home as here the days are still hot and sunny and the garden is full of bright flowers, butterflies and singing birds. We are really *very* lucky still to be here.
    Geoffrey and I have just been spending three hectic and gorgeous days in Hyderabad, Sind, where we used to live. We went to attend a large Hindu wedding, the eldest son of the 'Mukhi of Sind', and have been thrilled with every minute of it. We stayed with our host. All Indian houses seem to be vast affairs divided into self-contained flats, each with its own rooms, baths, showers etc., built around a small courtyard for the sons and their family as they marry. The one we were in could hold forty people. Patriarchal and keeping the money in the family! Our courtyard was the most charming little place, cooing pigeons above us, flowers and creepers in pots around the side and we sleep out in the centre of it at night under the intensely bright stars. The clear desert air makes them brilliant.
    We met the family for meals. They had Sindi food of course, not too highly flavoured, so that we liked it very much. The very *best* goat was in the curry. They ate everything with their fingers though we were given forks and it was an amazing sight to see dainty fingers laden with jewels — two of our host's single diamond rings

were half an inch across — dipping into the greasy curry. Silver bowls were brought, which I in my ignorance thought were for finger bowls but I was wrong. They *drink* from the silver bowls and so the old story is quite true, but the poor Shah, or whoever it is told about at Queen Victoria's dinner party, was only doing what he would in his own country!

After a day of garden parties and home festivities the Wedding day came. The procession through the famous Long Bazaar, which is hundreds of years old, is two and a half miles in length, and wide enough for one carriage and a cow, was about three-quarters of a mile long in itself. Geoffrey walked with the men while I was in a carriage drawn by two spanking chestnuts, silver collared and red and green feather plumes on their proud heads. Walking at our sides every few yards were men with great brightly coloured and painted lamps on their heads to light the way. When the gaslight started to grow dim they stopped and pumped it up with a tyre-pump and then rejoined the procession. Four bands were playing all the time, one in complete Highland uniform.

The ceremony at the Bride's House took ages but after the first half hour or so, when the bridegroom had had his feet washed in milk by his future mother-in-law and the bride had been fetched from an inner retreat and bride and groom were tied to each other by a crimson thread at the waist and had what looked like a muslin table-cloth tied around their waistline, our host took all of us who were in the front armchairs around the marriage dais to have drinks and cigarettes in another part of the house. The bride, by the way, was wearing the most *lovely* silver and chiffon sari, the edges deeply embroidered in pearls and diamenté. It was etiquette that she appeared weeping when led in by the groom but, as she is a modern educated and travelled girl, she just didn't raise a tear!

We only came back to the ceremony when it was nearly ended so that the boredom of Hindu weddings that people usually talk about was not ours. I had decided to wear my very best and scarcely worn satin and gold-thread gown I had from Harrods and a blue fluffy ostrich feather cape that is still holding together in spite of this climate. I was glad I did 'over dress' a little, as everyone's saris were so gorgeous and I was the only European woman there. I hear today that someone was told that a 'White English Rani was there'! As a souvenir they gave me a most lovely green gauze and gold-thread Benares sari and dressed me up in it after I had gone through the salt-tossing ceremony with the bride — that makes me one of the family; a nice gesture on their part. Some of the men wore European clothes and some Sindi costume, the high-necked white long coats fastened with jewelled buttons. Lots of the women, the older ones particularly, wore nose-rings, some so heavy that they bring a small strand of hair from their forehead to help hold up the ring.

Hyderabad at present is under martial law on account of the Hurs or armed bandits but it didn't seem to affect the wedding at all except that G. was obliged to carry a loaded pistol in his pocket all the time 'as Army regulations'.

Jacobabad

Karachi

I was going to tell you about our visit to Jacobabad. It is a small outpost on the Upper Sind border, founded by General John Jacob, just pre-Mutiny. He was a very wonderful soldier and administrator who put down the wild tribesmen and their raids, murders and general lawlessness, helped to irrigate the really vast desert and who created the Sind Horse. When he was Deputy Commissioner he and his men spent weeks in the saddle chasing the raiders over the desert until at last law and order and irrigation and British prestige ruled. They say that the Sind desert makes N. Africa look like a picnic! The old Residency, built by Jacob, is a vast old house with double verandas to try and keep out the burning heat. In March when we were there it was already uncomfortably hot and after this month the few women who are there have to leave their husbands and come to cooler climes.

Every year there is held the 'Week', which is a mixture of Horse Show and social gaiety. All the Sirdars, or heads of the tribes, and their followers come from the desert to buy and sell horses and some cattle and goats. They are most picturesque, wearing enormous turbans quite musical comedy in size, long long hair and flowing beards to match, then voluminous smocks to below the knee and yards and yards of Baluchi trousers, which are gathered in at the waist under the shirt, and red and gold pointed-toed shoes. They are all magnificent horsemen and ride fiery half-Arab stallions, usually bedecked with silver collars and bright beads and tassels. One that I sketched (he leaped a small hedge into the Residency garden as the Resident had met him in the road and thought I should like to see both horse and rider) had a high saddle and big silver stirrups like the film Mexicans! During the day we attended judging, prize-givings, Police Sports and races. At the latter the course of 1¾ miles is ridden bareback by wild and jungli jockeys (Oh! shades of Ascot!) and in the sports when the Sowars and Levies are competing in the tent-pegging, the hot air is rent with cries of old Islam 'Al-Al-Al-Allah', as against our own husbands and friends who screamed for 'George and Merrie England' as they thundered past. All great fun! Every night one of the hosts of the house-parties gave a dinner and dance, and for the whole week we never went to bed before 3 a.m. The last night was the most charming as the party was held in the historic Residency and we ate our dinner under the gaze of old John — he had a truly Biblical head, lovely black beard and beautiful eyes. In his spare time he constructed a big clock which shows the days and months and phases of the moon as well as hours and minutes. It stands in the hall and is still the timekeeper for Jacobabad! Its pendulum and weights are in a small pit and swing above a well of water so that the temperature doesn't alter much in the burning heat. General John's ghost walks the long veranda at night the most unimaginative people have seen him — but tho' I volunteered to stay up and watch for him, I was too tired when it came to the point. Heavens! *How* tired I was at the end of that Week! I've been recovering ever since!

Coming back we broke our journey to stay with friends in Sukkur and to see the huge Lloyd Barrage, which controls the entire irrigation of Sind and, in all, an area greater than the whole of Egypt. Sukkur used to be our farthest outpost and has an old mud fort on an island in the river. On another island is a sacred Hindu temple with wonderful marble carvings, age-old banyan-trees and screaming gaudy peacocks everywhere. We were taken over to it in a carved Indus ferry-boat, like a big gondola, and met on the steps by

Studies.

some priests, garlanded and made to take our shoes off and then shown around and given hotly spiced food to eat (a great honour). The food was served on 'plates' of leaves pinned together with thorns! To Sukkur come the grain boats from the Punjab, taking one month to come down and three to go back. They are flat-bottomed and have turned up noses like an Indian (or Dutch) shoe so that when they hit the crumbling banks of the Indus they push off easily and don't get embedded. The sterns and bulwarks are most beautifully carved and sometimes have pieces of mirror and gay tiles let in. You may have heard of the Sukkur Riots not long ago? It is not a very friendly place in the bazaar and we had a stone thrown at us!

Karachi in December

Sikh.

I sent off cards about two weeks ago and said I was writing this the next day but so much for my hopes. I then proceeded to get a bad attack of Denghie fever (the Americans call it 'Break-bone') and that's *just* what it feels like and this is the first day since that I've been able to get up and sit without pillows.

Today is quite the loveliest, just a cool tang in the air with singing birds and soft sunshine — it brings England back with a longing to be there, but I wonder when. As Geoffrey gets a few days' holiday just after Christmas we are going to pack up and go visiting, and leave our many cats, dogs, cows, horses, donkey etc., ad. lib. to be looked after by the servants. We have been to Jodhpur as you know but now think of going to Jaipur, which is an old historical town of Rajputana and then still further on to Udaipur which is supposed to be quite as lovely as a fairy-tale. Our Raja, Hanut Sing the polo player, has told us he will see that his friends and relations look after us and put us up and take us around, so I live for the day of our departure!

In the meantime, I am extremely busy drawing — either for Army propaganda, or else decorating walls for Clubs or Messes, all of which is great fun, if hard work. I think that I told you I had finished the four walls of the Indian General Hospital recreation room, which I decorated with figures just over four feet high. All were of Indians in the costume of their caste. One wall was of a Sindi fair — lots of lovely types and costumes there — another of S. India and two others of Rajputana, the sketches taken from the wedding processions etc., that we saw last February. It is all most colourful but unfortunately the rather bad photographs that were taken don't show it up properly. It is all so high up — my scaffolding was 18ft. high. The Hospital gave me a lovely little gold watch as present and the Gov. and the General etc., opened the room officially. Including

Seen at the Races.

the elephants and camels, I found I had painted 109 figures! Now I am to start the Karachi Gymkhana Club as soon as I feel strong enough to mount a ladder again. This will be just one huge wall on which I am splashing Spanish figures dancing etc. and generally making-merry at a fiesta — bull-fighting too — in a corner.

    In January comes the annual Horse Show at Jacobabad again but maybe we will not go this year — life is too short to do anything about more than once I find and I'm so afraid of spoiling my lovely memories of last year. It just *can't* be as good a second time! Since studying Spanish costume etc., for my next big work, I've learnt a lot about bull-fighting and when one knows more about it one comes to realise what a tremendous fascination it can have when performed perfectly — more like a superb ballet, perfectly timed, with a climax at the end of 20 mins. of ecstatic excitement. I *must* go to Spain, tho' I can well imagine that seeing one or two fights would not give one enough insight for *real* appreciation, anymore than two or three concerts can teach one the value of real music. 'Death in the afternoon' and one or two lesser known books on Spain have been absolutely enthralling me! One would just have to *not* look at the horses I suppose . . .

This evening I have been in the garden with G. picking out the best

pots of parchment coloured chrysanthemums for the house — the nights have suddenly turned cold and the flowers which are now in bud will all be killed I am afraid. On Monday we are having a tiny party; the General and his wife are coming and one or two other appreciative souls and I've got the 'Magic Man' as an attraction. He is just an itinerant Indian juggler whom I had in for sketching one morning but as I worked he started to do the most marvellous tricks which were quite as elaborate and sophisticated as any I've seen in London and so I have told him to come again for a Sahib's Party. Once I found some simply fascinating puppetry people whose dolls were all the old kings of India. The King of Delhi was quite superb with a big black beard and khol-lined eyes. They were all of carved wood, painted and dressed in the most gorgeous pieces of gold and satin. I asked lots of grown-ups to that party too. These childish things are always a success and so was my 'Snake party'. As people were sipping a gimlet they suddenly heard the snake-man's pipes and then I led them to a back veranda where the old ruffian had half-a-dozen of the most spectacular snakes popping out of baskets and crawling over the floor. It was really a screaming success, that party, and there are people who remember it yet!

Jodhpur
February

We went for ten days' leave to Jodhpur, and were lucky enough to be invited to the wedding celebrations for the Maharaja's eldest son. It was the fairy-tale India that one reads about but so very rarely finds. *The* most wonderful parties in the Palace, everyone a-glitter, real dancing-girls, each with her own musicians, one an accordion affair, one a drum and one a tooty-flute and the players get *so* worked up as they play, tho' the girl just postures nonchalantly and stamps her belled and jewelled feet occasionally. There is really very little movement in Indian dance, but *lovely* clothes and colours. The biggest party of all was given in the thirteenth-century Fort which crowns a great rock of sandstone. One winds up and up by car, and then at the Elephant Gates one goes on foot up a long ramp, the towers and terraces of the palace in the fort still above one. Here, on a flat marble rooftop decked with flags and lights, was the party. Every few minutes a bugle would go and as we looked over the edge we could see one raja after another being carried by eight palanquin-bearers up the ramp. The palanquins themselves were lovely — bright reds and greens inlaid with silver and gold. All the Indians were dressed in gold, red-shot-gold and yellow three-quarter coats (or achkans), tight trousers to the ankle, orange turbans (the marriage colour) and rows of medals and pearls and other jewels.

Facing page:
The Raja passes by.

There were twelve or so of the most important from all over India and the only two not dressed were Jaipur and Cooch Behar who were in Khaki uniform. Then came the biggest toots of all on the trumpets and the young bridegroom arrived carried in a pure silver palanquin and resting on pink cushions. He was dressed in gold and yellow and on his little crossed feet were jewelled slippers. I used to spend hours in the B.M. looking at the old Indian and Persian pictures and here it all was in real life!

After the reception, the First Minister, Sir Donald Field, the Resident and all the other European ministers and their wives and *us* waited until the torchlit procession had started. Looking down the ramp was just to see a stream of orange and gold wending its way, the bridegroom still being carried and followed by his charger in silver mail and all the other Princes and the Maharaja walking. The ladies were allowed to visit the zenana where the Maharani and all the old aunts, cousins and young girls were. Our shoes had to come off, and we all pattered across the marble courtyard, tripping over our best dresses. The Indian ladies were all in old Marwari costume which has a very wide skirt, little waistcoat and veil, and all made of the most lovely gold embroidered gossamery material you can possibly imagine. Ropes and ropes of pearls and emeralds and rubies wound round their necks and arms and ankles and the Marwari jewelled head-dress. The procession, which we all viewed from the roof of the royal Hindu temple in the old bazaar, took three hours to pass. We were at the Fort at 6.30 and left at 9 p.m. to go in cars to the procession. There was everything you had ever heard of — swaying elephants with gold-tipped trunks, painted faces and great tassels from their ears. Over their backs were age-old elephant-cloths of velvet covered in deep gold embroidery. The Mahouts were tossing money to the crowd and at one point I thought the people would be trodden on as they fought around the animals' feet! Then came camels, also clothed and decorated, with drums on their backs. They didn't seem to mind the bangs and booms, but went plodding on. Then the most glorious Rajput horses you can imagine, covered with silver and gold jewellery, each one having a BRACELET! Then all the State Forces, superbly mounted, lances high and then masses of people on foot, including the bevy of dancing girls and their music and then the Maharaja and the Princes, also on foot and then the bridegroom on horseback. It went on and on, amidst Indian music and cheers till at the very end came the modern armoured cars that H.H. has given for the War. There was almost too much to see and take in. I had a very front seat and sat sketching and making notes till I was weary. We got home well after midnight for a well-deserved supper. We were staying with the nice Rawlins — he is 'burra sahib' of the State Railway.

Next day the young Prince departed to collect his bride from a neighbouring state and there was an equally big party to see him off in his 42-coach train. His coach was white and gold, covered with flags and lights and marigold flowers and most of the Princes and his father and uncles went with him. The wedding was to be held

Snake-charmer.

in the bride's state and then they came back for more parties in Jodhpur a week later. G. and I couldn't stay for that.

Geoffrey was thrilled with the old buildings, all made from red sandstone and the new palace from pink sandstone. There are big quarries and one sees patient camels plodding along with a block or two at a time on their backs. Very little mechanical transport. Lovely shaped bullock carts. The animals have their long horns painted and beads tied on their necks too.

Karachi, Sind
May Day

What have I been doing? Well, two months ago I went to the annual Horse Show at Jacobabad, unfortunately without Geoffrey, who was too busy to take leave then — it was the same as last year only more so. The nightly dinner and dance parties took on a distinctly Chelsea aspect after 3 a.m., very gay. During the day there were the horses

'The Rock', near Sibi.

and sports, and all the fascinating long-haired Baluchis to amuse me. A few weeks afterwards I went to Sibi which is in Baluchistan before one reaches Quetta and reputed to be the hottest place. Here they were having a Political week, a Durbar with the new A.G.G. Col. Hay to take over. I stayed with the nice Alingtons — James is nephew of the Eton Alington — and had a really marvellous week. *Very* restrained and *no* wild parties but masses of gold braid, formal cocktail and luncheon parties and huge dinner parties — old official India at its best. I think I was asked because I draw, as I was the only non-Political there — again G. just couldn't make it and I was given the most advantageous seat at the Durbar for sketching *and* I made some good use of it. I had never before seen such amazing clothes as some of the old Bucti chiefs wore — seventy yards of white cotton material in their trousers and ballet-skirt shaped shirt and then at least twenty yards more on their heads as turbans and only a pair of eyes showing, as the rest of their hawk-nosed faces was covered with great black bushy whiskers and beards and long curls and flowing locks down to their waists, believe it or not!

Sibi itself is a small mud-walled town with a few political bungalows and is only used for about three months in the year by the Europeans as it is so hot, but the bazaar was most entrancing. There I saw some delightful Pathan boys with beautifully embroidered shirts. They looked quite Balkan, red and black stitching, and black pom-poms dotted about on the yokes and hems and lovely faded striped trousers underneath. Sir Benji Bromhead the Prop. Minister for Baluchistan took me about, as he is just as keen as I over the native costume. I had just about bought the shirt off a young Pathan's back — it was beautifully worked and I longed for it and it was reasonably clean — when someone in the inevitable crowd asked the bashful youth what he was going home in! And as, like all country people, they are extremely modest and shy, this awkward question just spoilt my chances of acquiring a unique smock, but Sir Benji said he would get a tribeswoman to make me one to my own measurements and I heard last week that I may expect it soon — it takes MONTHS of course and time is nothing to them, anyway.

A wonderful sight was the cattle at Sibi; enormous Indian bulls with great humps and exotic horns, all dressed up for show. Their coats (with a hole for the hump) were of rich silk and velvet, beautifully embroidered in glass mirror, beads and sequins, with tassels and flowers of every colour you can think of. They are not fierce like our bulls, and have great mild brown eyes like Jerseys. Usually they are pale in colour with darker markings for the head and hump. One of the exciting things was a ram fight — you could hear the impact of their heads for miles! Camel races were extraordinarily amusing, as the camel is a law unto itself! At night the tribesmen from the wilds gave dancing displays by the light of huge bonfires, then it seemed like the ballet from 'Prince Igor' as they leapt and waved their knives and shrieked in the firelight.

The Races

Sometimes we invite our friends from the Race Course and count ourselves honoured when the Rajput prince the Rao Raja Hanut Singh comes to our rather mixed gathering.

Apart from the horses, I am fascinated to see the wives and daughters of the rich Sindi Khans and merchants parading around the enclosure wearing their quite wonderful silk and gossamer-like saris which shimmer with almost unbelievable colours in the hot sunshine. Harsh crimsons and pinks, 'shouting' greens, violent lemon-yellows and cerulean blues, all besprinkled with a powdering of sun-catching glass beads and jewels, go to make a unique picture. Their black and shining hair with flowers tucked into the heavy chignon, their huge ear-rings and nose jewels as well as their ring-laden fingers display their family's wealth in no uncertain terms — and in the main, they are very beautiful women with the much-prized 'wheaten' complexion.

The Sindi men-folk accompanying the emancipated and glamorous ladies wear European suits of beautifully tailored cream or pale-coloured silk, topped with a panama hat and display flashing rings on their plump fingers.

Almost to vie with them are the jockeys, who have small circles of glass covering their Sindi-embroidered caps and the sun-flaps hanging over the backs of their necks; and I am sure, if they could, they would decorate their horses, too.

In the centre of the Course are the Race Officials, some European, some native, and all dominated by the compact form of the Rao Raja Hanut Singh and his incomparable Beryl. She is the slimmest of slim Anglo-Indians and as beautiful as a cat, with a smile that is sheer fascination. She has a wonderful seat on a horse, as well as great knowledge of the racing world, and the two of them are inseparable companions.

Very occasionally, Hanut's tiny and fragile-looking wife is there too, her bird-like fingers holding the edge of her exquisite sari which covers her head and most of her face. Beryl is chic in cool linen and her elegant suited figure stands out in the crowd of onlookers like a magnet — the East and the West for Hanut!

Americans in Karachi

March 1942

The U.S.A. has arrived! Strange accents and manners are everywhere, as the Americans seem to take over the town from superior Elphinstone Street to the Borhi Bazaar. Some of them look quite English, others Germanic, and still others have broad negro countenances: but all are prey for the beggars, the gharry-wallahs with their antiquated but still elegant Victorias drawn by horses bedecked with plumes and silver collars (the horse itself may be in almost the last stages of hunger and exhaustion, but the trappings are resplendent) and the shoe-shine boys. These latter low-caste urchins have quickly learned that no 'Americano' can clean his own shoes and so a vast and lucrative trade of shoe-shining goes on with the boys behaving like a quarrel-of-sparrows, and the Americans flinging wealth in the shape of uncalculated rupees at the noisy urchins. Never has Heaven been so near!

Shoe-shine.

The usual fare for a local ride in a gharry is about Rs.2, but these Americans, not knowing the language or custom, took the sum to be 'per person per trip' — at first, to the gharry-wallahs' infinite astonishment and delight — but they learned quickly and now each passenger pays the initial sum for the journey and so everyone is happy and the small beggars of 'baksheesh' follow the affluent soldiers, screaming and fighting to reach riches. This is all most astounding to the simple-minded British Tommy, who for generations has known the terse words for 'Go away' — 'Jao, baksheesh nai-hai, chello-chello' and so on.

Suddenly, amidst the din, around the corner with a deafening burst of noise, comes a high-powered motor-bike — and dressed in Army uniform with a hugely broad leather cummerbund, a negro rider, great cigar in his mouth and tiny 'fore and aft' cap on his woolly head, tears down the already much too noisy main street; times are changing!

Striking a bargain.

Lately, in liaison, we have come to know the officers of this astonishing Army and have invited them to our bungalow for the weekly parties we give, so that everyone can get to know everyone, to my great satisfaction.

On the morning of such a party there is a great 'haroosh' in the compound and through our 'IN' gate comes a great American Army truck. The driver's mate unloads large square cardboard crates to the astonished servants on the back veranda and the truck careers on, just missing the lame donkey, the half-dozen dogs and terrified cats who are dozing in the deep shadows of the Neem trees and so on to the OUT gate. When the crates are opened by the excited servants, many tins of American beer are found — this is the U.S.A.'s ever-generous contribution to tonight's party.

Baksheesh, and all that.

On the party evening, we put two of the charming 'lootenants' behind the little yellow bar to mix and serve drinks (during the week G. and I drink 'nimbu-pani' which is Urdu for lemonade, but at party times we bring out the gins and whiskies), and while G. goes around playing his banjo to our many friends and beguiling them with songs of the Deep South coal black mammies, the Welsh miners' laments and the country-fair ditties, I have time to circulate and talk with our guests.

P.S. to Americans in Karachi
This is a P.S. to these reminiscences — five years later when the war was over, we had a delightful letter from our American Colonel, who so often proppped up that yellow bar until the early hours of the morning. He writes 'I can still see that little bar and I wish we could all get together again and hear April tell her stories in that flat English brogue of hers. Gosh! how I used to love to hear her talk! She and Dorothy Ridley (who was the Chief Secretary of Sind's wife) used to be my idea of the finest England ever sent to India.' Dear 'Happy' — his other name was Clark and he was fat and jolly. I had no idea, when we know him, that he was listening so intently to my 'flat English brogue' and his letter amused us a lot.

Bangalore, Mysore State

I've owed you a letter for some time, but have been distinctly busy and lazy and so promised myself that you would be the first person I should write to once I'd arrived here. There was a great turmoil of packing up to leave Geoffrey in Karachi whilst I trecked for hundreds of miles down India to Mysore — you may have heard of it as the abode of a vastly wealthy Maharaja with modern tendencies and a backyard of fabulous palaces and jewels? Anyway, here I came last week, journeying a full seven days by boat and train and more train and yet more train — and India being what it is, never did any of the telegrams announcing my several arrivals all over the map reach those for whom they were intended. From the moment of my lonely landing in Bombay from the tender, surrounded by positive mountains of luggage (containing all my drawing-boards, easels, pounds of paint and masses of references, as well as clothes for six months) and having to try and control milling throngs of filthy and avaricious coolies, and (this was sheer inefficiency on Thos. Cook's part) there was no Cook's man to help me till I got to Bangalore at 7 a.m. after days and nights in the train and there was still no one to meet me or tell where to go in this vast and scattered city — I took it as all being good for my pampered character (Geoffrey has spoiled me quite a lot for self-reliance, he is so good at arranging things and getting everything done in a quiet way) and now to crown all I am living with five other WOMEN in a Red Cross bungalow; a thing that has never happened to me before! Most of them (they are Red Cross Welfare workers) have only recently come from home and are fresh and nice and not the rather hard-boiled gin-slinging type that India makes of nice young women after a few years. We all congregate for meals and I listen to stories of the Coventry Blitz and feel a worm of no understanding.

Did I tell you what I'm here for — MURALS! When Lady Louis Mountbatten and General Telfer-Smollett came thro' Karachi and saw my work there they evidently decided that I'd be useful in this huge 'Hospital Town' of Bangalore and so I was summoned down here. As all my expenses are being paid plus a small salary, I decided to leave my poor Geoffrey for a few months and come, as my adventures have been sadly lacking during the past two years and I do feel it's time I saw some more of Mother India before we leave. D'you know we may be home — almost *certainly* will be home, in the Autumn — I just can't believe it! But Geoffrey wants to know what the latest planning and building is and now that European V Day is declared he is due for demobilisation — I'm not sure that I want to come home to a damp and sun-less English winter. The heat and sunshine have got me — but if G. comes, of course, I will — and I do long to see you all more than anything else. Anyway, I've been taken around some of the buildings I am to ornament and instead of two or three months they surmised it will take me, I can see myself here for two or three years — there are twenty-one walls so far!

Bangalore is 3,000 odd feet above sea level; one comes up the most amazing ghats from Bombay to Poona. I thought of you continually, knowing how very thrilled you would be with the truly magnificent panorama; then two days of long plains with a few ranges in the distance — Sivaji's country where he and his 'Mountain Rats', as he called his Mahratta hill-men warriors, defied us and his hereditary enemies for years. As Karachi is practically below sea-level I feel a little 'high' at the moment! The greeness here is amazing after the deserts and there are lovely parks bordered with flaming red-flowered 'Flame-of-the-Forest' trees. They are huge and at their feet is a crimson carpet of fallen petals. Then there are pink-flowered acacias and intermingled are dark green banyan and mango-trees as a background. All *quite* exotic. The houses are of the old Indian type with big white Doric pillars and deep verandas — nothing modern concrete here thank Heaven! Shade and deep verandas and a minimum of glass are the essentials. I spent a night and a day in Bombay. Dined at the very famous and luxurious Willingdon Club where everything that can be mauve is, including the Bearer's dickeys! Lady Willingdon had a passion for mauve and even the débutantes had to wear mauve. On Sunday, motored out to the palm-fringed beach of Juhu, where Mr. Ghandi holds court to his worshippers from a basha on the beach. The surf was lovely and my friends had surf-boards to play with and the sea was *hot*. For drinks one buys fresh coconuts and has the top sliced off to make a cup and then we put ice into the coconut milk to cool it.

Karachi did its best with bright lights and flags and dances to celebrate V Day, but it was all a little flat — partly, I think, because in India there have been so few privations and sense of the European war and also because from this side we know the menace of Japan, still 'at large' and an enemy that will take a year or two yet to settle with. All I really wanted to do was to go to Church and say 'Thank God *some* of the horrors and slaughter are over' — which we did on Thanksgiving Sunday.

As I write I'm in the centre of a monsoon storm. The sky

was violet and copper and everything still. Then the trees started to quiver and wave a little and the sound of an express train steadily rushing towards one came and in two seconds the trees were a whirling mass, bowing to the ground. Flowers and leaves swirled around the garden and all the doors and windows banged at once — and now there is torrential rain to the grumbling of thunder and dashing steel of lightning; *exciting!* This is the end of the hot weather season and every afternoon at 5.30 we have bad thunder and rain but nothing like this storm have I seen before.

Bangalore
August 4th

Shall I tell you a tale of witch-craft — true, because I saw it? The only trouble is that it is hard to recapture the eerie atmosphere and evil fear and it won't sound nearly as gruesome as it looked on a dark night!

Not far from here is a small lake. In the daytime it always reminds me of Rydal Water — the reeds come down to the edge of the water and trees grow near by on the green banks. At one end is a promontory which is very rocky and at the top there's a Hindu Temple. It can just be seen between the trees and this little bit is very 'holy'. A naked and ash-smeared 'sadhu' with his 'chela' live in a tiny cave near the road and there is a shrine which day and night has a lamp burning before the god. Big pepal and banyan trees border the road there too — *very* holy. One dark and almost moonless night I was coming back from a dance and my escort suggested we came around by the lake. We heard a really shocking din in the distance and at first I thought it was a wedding celebration. As we got nearer there was the beating of the drums and the shrieks and yells sounded most un-cheerful. Around the bend under the trees was a vast crowd of men and boys holding torches and shallow basins of fire and those in the front of the crowd kept rushing up to the trunk of the tree with the flames. We stopped the car and then I saw a woman, a sagging heap of unconsciousness, propped against the big tree trunk. My first idea was that they were going to burn her and that she must be rescued (*don't* laugh! I forgot for the moment there were only two of us to a big crowd). The air was thick with smoke and flame, the beating of the drums and the screams and yells of about fifty people, then I saw that they were nailing the woman to the tree by a hank of her long black hair. Still the drums throbbed and they threw ashes or something powdery at her as she was suspended by her hair and then I rushed forward with a feeling that I must save her. Then with an extra piercing shriek the foremost man made a grab at her, tore her away from the nail leaving a great hank of black hair dangling and slung her over his shoulder and the whole lot went loping and scampering off into the darkness in an ectasy of noise. We could watch the torches and flares going up the boulder-strewn goat track of the hill side, flickering through the trees and so to the temple at the top until all that remained was the sense of evil and the throbbing of the drums. My escort held back a straggler who had stayed to look at us, otherwise I don't think anyone had noticed us though I was in the thick of the crowd at one moment trying to get to the woman until Larry pulled me back — and this man told us that the woman was a witch and had an evil spirit which they were casting out. They would have further ceremonies up in the temple with the priest; then they'd leave her on the tomb all night — (there was such a feeling of horror everywhere that I shouldn't have been surprised if they ended by making a true human sacrifice while they were at it!). Anyway, that was that and afterwards I suddenly felt quite frightened and even Larry, a large six-footer with three years in Burma and jungle war-fare with the Japs, said he felt distinctly shaken — that is the other side of the Indian picture! The day after we passed the same place in the sunshine of the morning and there was the black hank of hair still hanging from its nail but all was quiet and the lake in a peaceful ripple and the 'sadhu' had a piece of old sacking over his cave door which no doubt signified 'Not-at-home'.

Another time, by myself, in a Victoria with a venerable old grey-beard as coachman, I came thro' a small village and saw over the roofs of some little houses a grove of palm trees and a huge Hindu Temple, towering high above everything and most ornately carved. I told 'Buddah' to take me there and we went down a few filthy but colourful side-streets and came across a most amazing place. Hundreds — possibly thousands — of almost life-sized figures, carved out of stone, all over the temple gateway, and near by, under a modern brick archway, an enormous juggernaut car with colossal wooden wheels. No doubt its resting place in between processions when it would be decked out with all the gold and silver and gaudy colours imaginable. The wheels would easily crush a bullock, let alone a human, I should think! I'm told that the populace no longer hurls itself under the wheels in an ecstasy of annihilation but after my little witch-craft stage-set I'm prepared for anything. I've seen Mohammedans in the Muharram festival beat their naked bodies with tiny knife-edged flails as they whirl and twist and call upon the names of the 'Martyred Brothers' and others who, taking a piece of flesh on their breast, pierce it through with short skewer-like swords until their chests are a mass of raw flesh — and I'll swear they don't feel a thing. I can go on being gruesome for quite a long time more — but I *won't*.

To Geoffrey

Bangalore

Your telegram was delivered at 1.30 a.m. and somebody who was still here and making merry decided I must be awakened. Thank you

— I now wait with 'baited breff' for the promised letters and the answers to all my questions. There is a most ridiculous 'Woolly-Dachs' puppy playing around my feet, a pet of a thing which belongs to one of the girls but as I'm in and she is out nearly all the time it rather attaches itself to me and gives shrill and piercing small barks for food if it's hungry. Otherwise it says little but chews — *chews*. At the moment it is busy on the leg of a wicker chair which is preferable to my light's flex, shoes and leather writing-case — all of which have had its attention in the last ten minutes. So I'll let it be, it's full of MILK — my life is always bounded by saucers of milk it seems! There is a possibility that I acquire a Siamese lady and her Child (CATS). They are about to be deserted as the owner is going to England and I'm lonely. D'you think it would be wise? I am sorely tempted. Heavens! the minute *spot* of a dog is pulling a really large wicker chair along the veranda at high speed! Too funny! And one of my Bat People has come back and is hanging upside down looking at me — rather intrigued with George (the puppy) I think.

Today I have at last finished the first wall. It has taken me a long time because there are a lot of figures and background and two windows at the top which they wouldn't have blocked up and so the light threw all my balance of colour out and I've positively toiled and moiled. The General seems very pleased and Air Vice-Marshal Thornton came in today to inspect and was most intrigued and went out muttering that he envied me a lot — he is nice!

Bangalore
July 9th

My Woolly Dog, a stray who came to stay, is now so thoroughly domesticated and sure of himself that he guards the house and barks at the other pi-dogs and Indian udmys (true to type!). He is brushed and combed each day by me and he simply adores it — but he is distinctly jealous of George the small puppy of whom I did you a small-sized sketch and just now, when I put George on my knee as I was writing, Woolly, who was at my feet, got up and, putting his hands on the chair, took poor little George by the scruff of the neck and tried to drag him to the floor!

This afternoon I went out to the shops and came back in a gharry to save money as taxis are so costly. The gharry horses here are vast — have to be eighteen hands by law — but there are only three or four of them and the gharry-wallahs look like decayed Bearers and wear dirty white with a brass number plate on their cummerbunds and on their pugaree. This poor wretch I had took about half an hour to get out here and would only go when whipped — so of course I arrived like Boadecea whip in *my* hand. I then got Paul to give it a bucket of water while I looked at its feet. While all this was happening, half the inmates of the bungalow had collected. One thought the horse was being sick as I was holding a bucket under its mouth. Another remarked that I hadn't been in time (the horse had made the usual puddle!) and another said was I going to bath it or ask it in to tea! So you see the reputation I have. Incidentally, I found a whopping inch-square of granite in the poor beast's hoof, so of course it couldn't trot. I will say it looked well fed and it wouldn't drink any water. The tiny tonga ponies are just about the size of Great Danes but all seem in good condition. In fact the animals here are all right but the people a poor lot.

The bullocks are much smaller than the Sindi ones and have different shaped horns which are painted blue or red or green and have knobs with bobbles and tassels at the end. The oddments are all brass and the tassels red wool — rather delightful — but I don't seem to be able to draw bullocks very successfully, do I?

Bangalore

I must tell you about yesterday when we came out and no doubt the 'Bundobust King' will smile his gentle mocking smile while he reads!

Here they provide everything except food — no need to bring sheets or skeeta-nets or anything. So Peg and Bill (whom I'm chaperoning in the most perfect way possible my love — as only a woman of my outlook can, if you understand!) said they would make all arrangements about bringing food. All I'd to do was to pay my share of the bill and not worry. The car was to be at Primrose Road at 11 a.m. and I was all ready. There is a rule that no taxi can go further than ten miles out of Bangalore and this is twenty miles out — so Bill had arranged with a Contractor to supply a car. The tins and stores of bread and suitcases of Peg's and Bill's were vast and bulky. All I had was a bistra with a blanket and pillow (I trust nobody) and a pair of slacks and a dressing-gown and my portfolio — but the car supplied had no Boot and a tiny, tiny carrier at the back so we had to sit three at the back, with luggage piled all around us and Paul, my young Bearer, was next to the driver holding my portfolio while the driver had his right arm thro' the window holding on to the spare tyre as the string to hold that on was supporting a vast suitcase on the right hand wing! Talk about a CIRCUS being moved...!

Well — we started. None of us had been here before, nobody even had a map, but the Contractor said the driver knew the way and that it was about twenty miles up the Mysore-Ooty Road. After ten minutes the driver asked Bill the way. Bill wasn't sure, so the driver got out and asked a woman selling peanuts, a small boy and finally a peon got in and off we went — and *on* we went, and *on* we went. At the eighteenth mile stone we told him to stop and ask a labourer. At last there was a sign-post saying to some reservoir — an appalling road all pot-holes and I felt simply frightful with nausea but the thought of our destination and a good lunch buoyed me up and so we banged and bumped till we reached a lakeish-looking place and Bill got out terribly and awfully stiff to ask where the Inspection Bungalow was while Peg and I admired a small and very sweet steam-roller that was having its chains cleaned and I discovered that she has a real passion for them too. Anyway, after ten minutes or so Bill and the driver came back and believe it or not — and you will — we had spent from 11.30 to 1.30 and God knows how many gallons of petrol coming twenty-five miles in the *wrong direction* and back we had to go, all the way to Bangalore and start again! If only Bill had at least looked at a map — and d'you know the driver said 'Oh yes, he knew the Reservoir, that wasn't it, but the Sahib had said Mysore Road and he had come on the Mysore Road, but he knew the Inspection Bungalow at 'Chaimarajah Pet' and of course that wasn't it!' Can you beat it! Bill nearly beat him — and so back we went all over this frightful road to the main road and then ate a few biscuits as it was nearly 2 p.m. and we'd had no lunch. Then the driver started to argue and said it wasn't the Contractor's car 'It was *his* car and the Contractor had told him it would only take him the morning and now he was going back to Bangalore' and he waved his flopping hand at us — the other still out of the window holding the spare wheel — so the car just went on by the grace of God.

When we'd done the whole mileage back and were practically where we started from, Bill stopped the car, tested the petrol (the Moron said he'd no more petrol anyway! my foot) — and then called a policeman who brought a pal — and then the *whole* of the town collected and Peggy and I felt we'd like a purdah veil as there were so many faces peering in. Anyway, after a vast amount of insulting remarks had been passed on all sides the driver climbed in again. He had a mop of long greasy hair, a fur hat, a dirty blue shirt and very short shorts. He took off his hat, he took off his shirt and I thought he was going to take off his shorts too, but he left them on, and off we started at breakneck speed for the other direction. We arrived here at 5.30 and we could have arrived at 1 p.m. as it is only twenty miles and quicker and nicer to reach than the first place we went to. It just shows we should look at a map first and not trust the driver at the wheel.

Victory Day in Karachi, 1945

There has been an incident which has had us all laughing — I must tell you. As you may guess, all kinds of small irregular attachments have been going on, but as discreetly as maybe, and blind eyes have been turned on the lonely young officers and their alluring girlfriends. One of the latter was known as 'The Passionate Haystack' because of her mop of yellow hair — but no one quite knew about the rest of her life.

So you may imagine our amusement when, as the town's procession and the marching troops, bands, banners and flags were passing a large block of balconied flats facing the Victory Parade route, there on one of the lower balconies stood a well-known scion of a famous confectionery firm in his purple and white striped pyjamas, military moustache and hair waving in the breeze, with his arm across the shoulders of The Passionate Haystack, who was clad in the most revealing of diaphanous nightgowns, both waving excitedly to the crowds down below — all at about 3 o'clock in the afternoon. I believe there was even some chat about this 'public event' in the Club afterwards — but I laughed and laughed, as we all did; life is too short for much else.

Sandspit

And I laughed again one Sunday morning out on the island of Sandspit, where everyone who could sail spent the weekend. We were guests of Toni the Greek — a handsome and lithe charmer, representing a famous firm of tobacco merchants — and his current girlfriend, Estelle. But alas! from almost nowhere, there had arrived in Karachi a most wonderfully fascinating, fortune-hunting red-head, and the Demon Lover (as G. facetiously named our really kind and good friend Toni) couldn't possibly resist this new allure, who by some strange stroke was also at the bathing weekend hut and had Toni quickly enslaved by her unusual beauty. Estelle, with her long, long honey-coloured hair and madonna-like face was totally eclipsed for the time being and I watched with fascination as she set about getting her man back. First, down came the hair — so long that she could sit upon it — then out came a comb and she proceeded to stroke and arrange the heavy strands, all the while leaning this way and that in her brief 'bather', humming little tunes and making seductive gestures with her beautiful arms until Toni just had to take notice of her. Once the rapport was established, she almost crooned the sad story of how she had left her husband and two little children for love of this Greek and was now a lonely and pathetic girl, entirely dependent upon the kindness of others — and this she knew she could have from countless admirers, but her heart was rent and almost broken. Then came more combing of her lovely hair and the madonna face — such a contradiction of her real nature if the truth were known — was bedewed with tears, as the blue, blue eyes with their long black lashes looked at the now embarrassed lover.

I, of course, was entranced with all this soulful drama and really did hope she might win this highly feminine battle, and she did — and by the next day they were at the Club dancing and Estelle had yet another model gown to make us envious.

Toni simply couldn't resist pretty women and told a story against himself of how, walking along in front of him in the

Camels at Sandspit.

main shopping street, there was a young woman with a wonderful back view and legs and ankles more delightful than he had ever seen. He followed, caught up and passed her, giving a casual kind of glance so as not to embarrass her, and found, to his amusement, that the fair lady was his own sister, not so often seen in the gay social whirl.

The clash

When the Major's tough little wife had notice that he was 'missing, presumed dead,' she wasted no time on tears but organised her roomy house into a weekend Guest House, plus every want supplied for the young officers who cared to be her P.G.s — and so for a while, blind eyes were turned and no one was hurt.

One of the daytime delights she provided was to take a motorboat-load of gay young people out to Sandspit, everyone bringing pies, hams, chickens and drinks, as instructed — and so enormous was the amount of food left over and put back in the boat's iceboxes that the thrifty widow had enough for herself and her family for the rest of the week. She had a younger and very attractive friend who helped her in all these enterprises, but alas! the friendship came to an abrupt end one evening after a gay day's outing finished at the Boat Club for dancing; and these two women became jealously possessive of one of the young officers, who, in company with everyone else, had had rather too many drinks.

The quarrel for possession went on over his bowed head as he sat at a table — and suddenly, nobody knowing who struck the first blow, the two ladies started to fight. It was all most shameful and seniors quickly restored order and the offending parties were taken home. The next day, and for a few to come, the bruised cheeks and truly shocking black eyes were there for all to see.

We were all very glad when one day the missing Major, whom everyone liked and respected, suddenly arrived in time for breakfast in his own home — and the fateful telegram was put down to a War Office mistake.

Secunderabad-Hyderabad, Deccan

This is a lovely place in parts — Muslim city of Hyderabad, quite Arabian Nights in conception — great white buildings topped with 'onions' and minarets — the bazaar, tho' new (comparatively), with great wide streets and tremendous arches which make lovely vistas and still retain an Eastern feeling in a most decided manner. Tho' there are no stinks such as Calcutta specialises in and which seem generally inseparable from anything Indian, the crowds dressed in achkans and tarbushes, the bullock-drawn carriages so reminiscent of the old illustrations to 'Kim' and above all the many mosques can never for a moment be confused with anyting modern.

We took a car and penetrated to the eastern city beyond a lake, with its surrounding hills dotted with white palaces, houses and the inevitable clusters of minarets. Amongst other things, I have never seen so many Pathans out of Baluchistan, and we had great fun buying some ornamented sandal-wood combs, made in Khabul, from an old and rascally Afghan. He sat on the pavement under a colonnade, his wares spread out before him, and his choicer specimens in an old camel bag by his side. His fellow country-men, with their oily bobbed hair, impertinent moustachios and beards, surrounded us like flies after sugar to see that the deal was well done and they one and all helped with the bargaining, some on our side! Of course, no English was spoken and they loved Geoffrey's Urdu and my more hesitant attempts, especially when I told them that I had been to Afghanistan and seen the great baggy trousers, gay long shirts and small ornamented waistcoats. It all seemed like being in Quetta again.

The predominating colour that the Hyderabadi wears seems to be a lovely crushed strawberry and crimson and the men wear beautifully cut long coats, very waisted and having enamel buttons down the front, with great aplomb and a swagger. We found a small shop with boys moulding and blocking tarbushes on the doorstep outside and then went in and saw the entire shop's shelves covered with small hatboxes, each one containing a tarbush. The colours varied from the more usual bright red to lovely wine colours and deep maroons and as I have always wanted a real one, I thought I couldn't do better than buy one in a Muslim city, from a shop that imported them direct from Egypt and so now I own a wine-red tarbush, complete with black silk tassel, lined with exotic cerise silk — *and* what is more I intend to wear it when I get home!

The cantonment of Secunderabad is rather like any other we have seen, nicer than Bangalore perhaps, but similar; and the race-course is just across the road from this hotel but like the Maidan in Calcutta, covered with bashas and tents and junk. We have joined the Secunderabad Club which is a nice old place and owns the Sailing Club by the lake and we intend to do as much sailing as we can in the next few days.

The bazaar of old Secunderabad, being a British Cantonment, has not suffered from the replanning and cleaning that Hyderabad has and there are some quite fascinating alleys and quarters to sketch. The little white houses swarming with children and dogs and old women have heavy wooden doors ornamented with huge brass knobs every six inches or so and verandas and woodwork painted a heavenly turquoise blue — doorways seem to be mainly terracotta or ochre and the letter boxes are all yellow too. I could stay here for ages.

Golconda

We have been to see the Fort of fabulous Galconda, which rises high from the plains of marshes and small lakes. Now it is battered and old but the big elephant gates, covered with knobs and spikes against attack, are still most formidable and a small company of State troops is still housed there. On the crumbling bastions are antique guns and huge cannon balls made of solid stone, cleanly piled in pyramids and now kept as souvenirs.

The moat is overgrown and small trees perch on the battlements but once the Kings of Hyderabad lived in Golconda and there are big houses and mosques and temples within the walls. The citadel is reached by stone steps blasted from the rocks and boulders that crown the hilltop which has small castellated towers precariously clinging to every overhanging corner. Great wells, forty feet square, are still filled with scummy water and our guide, an officer of the

State Forces, told us that they are some hundred feet deep. I can't think how anyone *ever* took the Fort from the defenders, but it did happen once, owing to a clever trick on the enemy's part — but even then they only got to the outer walls and never to the citadel.

The ground around, on the plain, is pitted with holes and caverns where the mines for gold and diamonds have been worked and there is a law that no one may start digging anywhere without permission from the Nizam (which is always refused!) in case the casual diamond is unearthed. While we were in the region of the Fort we were taken over the paddy-fields which skirt the walls, to see the 'Biggest Tree in India' — not, as I thought, in breadth of foliage, but girth of bole. It is, believe it or not, ninety feet around and the single trunk grows up for nearly twenty feet before it widens out into four huge and gnarled branches. The centre is hollow, tho' one has to climb high to look down into the cavity. The whole thing is some monstrous freak of nature, as the wood of the tree seemed more like polished lava than anything else, bulging and bubbling in a most unorthodox manner! Our Indian car driver, who came with us, piously preserved a cluster of leaves to take home to his family, as he said it was a 'very holy' tree. Out here *anything* that is odd is holy, from deformed animals, upwards!

Waltair

Coming back, as the train changing was awkward and I hate getting up at 3 a.m. to sit about a cold and draughty station, we spent the night at a little place called Waltair, which is the station for the port of Vizagapatam, the naval base. We reached our little hotel after everyone had gone to bed and Geoffrey had to prod the night-watchman or Chokidar *heavily* to awaken him and ask where our room was. He, the Indian protection against thieves, ye Gods! We looked over the blue bay and we had the sound of waves with us all night — lovely. It is a small and amusing place with two or three little houses and hotels practically on the beach, as we discovered next morning, and the bluest of seas comes roaring and roistering up the beach to the palm trees and the Marsula [mussoola] boats that the fishermen leave hauled up when they are out in their catamarans — or perhaps I should say *on* their catamarans, as they are merely three pieces of light-weight wood about four feet in length, which they tie together with a piece of palm rope when they want to fish from them; otherwise the pieces of wood are just left about the beach loose. The Marsula boat, which dates back centuries without any alteration in its construction, is an amazingly simple piece of work — just thin planks with holes bored at each edge to take palm rope about as thick as an electric light flex, this is 'sewn' thro' the holes, with more palm fibre as caulking, so that the whole boat is flexible; not a nail or

Mussoola boat.

pin anywhere. The prow is high, a little like an old Norse boat, and in the thunderous waves the whole thing about 30 feet long, rides like a cork, where a more rigid type would be battered to pulp in no time.

Calcutta

I must tell you about Calcutta—the biggest, most important and filthiest of all the cities in India. Now I have seen them all: Bombay, Karachi, Lahore, Delhi, Agra, Amritsa, Madras and Calcutta, and Karachi is the cleanest and this is the dirtiest!

Here, at every street corner and half way along the side streets, are placed large galvanised DUST-BINS and they are open to the air, to the cows and kites and pariah-dogs, to the rats and cats and beggars. During the day, some of all these tribes are rooting in the vast bins—in fact no cow in this country seems to eat anything except garbage and paper. None of these puts back that which they have clawed out as they look for morsels, so that the pavement for three feet in all directions is littered with every kind of stinking—stinking, I repeat—rubbish, from melon rinds to very highly dead dogs—and to say that to pass a garbage-bin makes one feel sick and choking is to put it mildly. Now do not blame the poor British for this; Bengal has its own native government and municipal councils—ugh! Not long ago, one morning, Geoffrey had to spend quite a lot of time telephoning the police and God-knows-who to try and get the dead body of a man removed from the side of the road where it was lying, as it was nobody's in particular's business to see to it.

The streets near the river and the railway station, where I arrived, are indescribably sordid, broken with vast pot-holes, narrow, with tramlines in the centre, and filthy to the last imaginable degree. Take the most depressing back streets in Birmingham or Stockport, make them unspeakably filthy and lined with great stinking garbage-tins, their contents spread all over the pavements and road, and you have my first impressions of Calcutta.

After the most appalling traffic jams, which involve huge lorries, trams, taxis and both bullock-carts and coolie-drawn carts, one comes to the lordly Clive Street in which are all the big shipping and business houses and everything is on a much grander scale—but still the garbage-tins—and then comes Chowringhee, with the Maidan on one side and rather super-looking trams running in a grass verge among the trees—that is charming—but still the garbage-tins—and off that is Park Street with its delightful houses and flats and old cemeteries dating back to 1750-odd and Theatre Road, where we are now living. The latter has charming houses and the street is bordered with flaming orange canna lillies just like a park, but still the garbage-tins as well of course. Everywhere there are trees—big ones. I have never seen so many in a city and they give lovely shade and make everything look cool and delightful.

Park Street Burial Ground.

In all other Indian cities that I have been in, and in Madras particularly, there is an Eastern air to the buildings with deep verandas built out from the houses, but here in Calcutta there is no outward concession to the East at all and the houses all look as tho' you were in Westbourne Terrace, London. But once you are inside, of course there are huge cool verandas and masses of electric punkas. Perhaps Cheltenham is the nearest parallel, especially at night. The dark comes on about six o'clock and the lamplighter, clad in dhoti and little Hindu hat, plus the black umbrella that no respectable Bengali is seen without, and accompanied by his ladder-carrier, goes around to all the gas lamp-posts with a box of matches and lights up!

Fort William, where the British first started their trading in the early seventeenth century, is not nearly so fascinating as Fort St. George of Madras, or as old, as the original fort was quite destroyed and this only dates from Clive and Plassey. The Black Hole is also no more, but there is a monument to the ghastly episode (which, incidently, the natives say never happened and was only imagined by the British. Anything an Indian doesn't like he just denies the existence of and that's that!)

Kali's Temple

You have probably heard of the Goddess Kali the Destroyer. It is said that the original name of Calcutta was Kalighat, but I'm not sure if it is correct. Anyway, Kali's Temple and the Burning Ghats are at Alipore, a little way from here, where the old British merchants had their 'garden houses' as the country houses were called. Chowringhee is the way to Alipore, and originally was a pilgrim path thro' the tiger and panther infested Maidan. A pious Hindu called Chowringhee made it his good deed to the goddess to keep the path cleared and the forest trimmed back a little, so that the pilgrims, some of whom had come from the other end of India and possibly not on foot only, but laying the *whole length* of their bodies along the roads and the journey taking years (they still do it!) should not, in their last stages, be snapped up by some hungry tiger.

At Alipore there is a tributary of the sacred Ganges, crossed by a small and rather rickety bridge and the first iron-span bridge built by the British, incidentally. The banks of the river are of slimy brown mud and the water the thickness of the mud on a Manchester street on a wet day. On the other side is a temple of Shiva, and wide steps come down to the river's edge so that the pious and bereaved may immerse themselves in the holy filth. It is not a particularly imposing temple — I have seen much more ornate and bigger ones many times but it is old and incredibly greasy and dirty and I suppose that is enough. First one comes to a wood-yard. Here lie great piles of faggots, branches and trunks of trees and beside them a ramshackle hut in which a fat Hindu sits cross-legged, selling the fuel for the cremations.

It was evening when we went there and there were crowds of men, women and children milling around doing nothing in particular. We passed the steps of a modern building of concrete near by and there was an Indian orchestra — tom-tom, flute and portable harmonium, playing songs and droning the words — while a group of women, mainly oldish, sat about and chatted; our guide said they came every evening, just a matey get-together for the old ladies who weren't dead enough to be on the fires yet. We wended our way thro' them and followed him into a great square under the walls of Shiva's temple, which was completely surrounded by a high brick wall. From the outside we had seen smoke and flames and wondered if we should be allowed in, but the guide nearly dragged us in, he was so keen that we should see the famous Burning Ghat. So — being thrust into the wall compound, we looked around. There were four different pyres about three feet high built over shallow holes and four bodies were being burnt. One fire was nearly out and the relatives were squatting around waiting to collect the ashes to throw them upon the river outside; another corpse was half consumed with only the head left. As this was not being burnt quickly enough, somebody came with a bamboo pole and pushed it farther into the flames, in a most casual manner. One had just been lighted and the bright hot flames and smoke were keeping people at a distance, while the fourth had not yet been lighted and the relations were processing around the pyre and chanting. Near us, just left against the wall was the body of an old man, not even half-covered with a piece of cloth. There was nobody with him, or with another body on a charpoy a little farther on — a strange sight, just left by the wall-side alone.

Around us stood men and boys, young women with babies, old women and small grandchildren, pi-dogs snarling and scratching, cows, calves and crows, and everywhere the shrill voices of the crowd, the crackle and smoke of burning wood and the faint echo of the Indian orchestra behind the temple. There was absolutely *no* air of reverence or of sorrow or bereavement — a market-day couldn't have seemed more casual. To me, it seems slightly horrible to think that I am on the very spot where so many ghastly ceremonies have taken place, before the British had put a stop to Suttee, or the burning alive of the man's widow. Apparently, altho' she was supposed to fling herself onto the funeral pyre of her own free will, she was in reality *tied down* to the corpse and a rope was fastened to the four corner stakes of the pyre. Then she was well sprinkled with oils and fats and covered with straw and when the eldest son had lighted the first faggot, two men relatives kept the poor stupefied woman 'in place' with long wooden poles, in case she got away.

I have never forgotten a thing I saw in Jodhpur. On the wall of the Fort gate and again on the walls of the City gate that led to the old Burning Ghats were the impresses of many tiny hands, now gilded over and protected from the weather. These were the last impressions of the little Rajput widows as they were carried out to be burnt on their dead husbands' funeral pyres — and I don't think I have ever seen anything more pathetic.

Well, after this, let me continue about this gorgeous East. Having fallen over rubbish, old tins, dirty paper and fruit skins on our way out past the tomb-tablets of departed Rajas (equivalent to our graveyard), all incredibly filthy as usual, we said 'Now show us the world-famous temple of Kali the Destroyer', so our guide led us thro' village streets by the riverside for about half a mile. Here there were hundreds of people taking their evening stroll, buying pan and dhal at the little poky hole-in-the-wall-shops that constitute an Indian bazaar and just generally idling about with their wives and children.

At last, in front of us was the Temple of Kali — just another dirty old building, without any of the outward glamour that one might expect. We entered with the crowd thro' a little much-rubbed door and found ourselves in a narrow alley. On either side, raised a few feet from the ground were little shops, the stone slab providing a place for the owners to sit and to display garlands of flowers, leaves covered with berries and pieces of pink melon. Men, women and children in a perpetual stream were passing in and out of this very narrow passage the whole time and a rivulet of *very* dirty water ran at their feet. Set back on the stone slabs opposite the 'shops' were shrines to the various gods and goddesses, guarded by their priests. One frightful old thing set up a howl like a jackal when he saw us and waved and gesticulated to his tinsel-decked Kewpie dolls, who represented some Hindu deities. Don't be shocked, nearly half the deities are in reality, to us, Kewpie dolls. The lovely little marble temple on the Peacock Island of the Indus at Sukkur had two outsize Kewpies as Ram and his consort and *great* homage was paid to them by our Western-garbed, Western-educated host. We shied off these and a few others and were jostled down the narrow alley, past a big island of a shrine where a circle of young and old women were processing, their children with them, around and around to a monotonous chant. This was saying 'thank-you' to the goddess of Fertility for the offspring they had. At the base of this shrine was a small hole, about a foot across; as the passing multitude came to this, they dipped their hands into the dirty reddish-brown water it contained and poured it into their mouths. Our guide said that inside the shrine was a figure of the goddess and over her ran this filthy gory-looking water, and thence to the outside puddle — very, *very* holy. What about cholera, typhoid, dysentery, etc.?

    A little farther on at a corner was another slab from which grew a small stunted tree, the trunk quite black and the gnarled branches hanging with small pebbles and pieces of brick, tied thereon by string and ribbon. Up and down the trunk crawled quite the nastiest and most repulsive black lizard I have *ever* seen — usually I like lizards but seeing this one made me ill. In front were two stones smeared with red paint, representing the 'Female emblem'. All alone by the side of this most repulsive shrine sat a very young girl dressed in her wedding clothes and with the saddest little face possible. She was a 'barren wife', thereby almost an outcast and this shrine was her last hope. She had first bathed in the river and taken from it a small stone to hang on the tree and she was now making her supplications to the Goddess of Fertility. In all probability her husband was some nasty old man, beyond anything in the family way. Having made suitable donations to the temple, when the night came, some priest would take her and after all she would have a child — the sole function of a Hindu woman — her prayers had been answered; just too simple! I can still see her sad little face as she sat bowed beside this horrid black and stunted tree; black, because when a child is born, the mother hangs a lock of it's black hair on the slimy trunk.

    The dirty water was making my toes wet, so we moved on and came to an open stone courtyard. At one side there were planks of wood with wide notches cut into the top and here every morning are made the living sacrifices to Kali, whose shrine is in this courtyard. In the old days one could kill anything one liked for a sacrifice and I shouldn't wonder if a few humans were not included — only WOMEN if there were, of course — but now-a-days they only go in for goats. There was a nasty smell and a lot of gory stains around and three women were squatting at wooden blocks, busy cutting up some remains of flesh and putting them into separate bowls which would be distributed to the needy pilgrims. The heads were not cut and could be bought by the pious rich. Pi-dogs in every state of disease sat scratching alongside them and kites wheeled overhead mewing; babies crawled in and out of it all. Strange ash-smeared Sadhus, with the sign of Kali on their foreheads and carrying a kind of trident, hung about, watching the proceedings; rasp-voiced vendors of red garlands and sweetmeats added to the noise. The ever-flowing stream of dirty water seemed really useful for once and it washed away the blood and mess.

Coming back, in the almost-dark, the smoke and flying sparks from the Burning Ghats lit up the palm trees beside the river banks and made the old temple of Shiva almost beautiful against the dark blue skies and as we crossed the river by the dicky bridge (which I am certain will collapse some day and fling them all into the filthy stream below) we could just hear the small thin sound of the flute and drum, and India seemed to have regained her magic for me again.

Poona

You may have read that India is expecting another famine (that hasn't prevented the rioters from burning and destroying a vast amount of stored grain, both in Calcutta and here). Coming through E. Bengal in the train last week we were appalled at the state of the land and the cattle. The monsoon having failed, vast tracts of land were already parched and brown where they should be green with growing rice and grain. Small rapidly-drying ponds didn't look as tho' they would be even damp patches in a month's time and all the cattle were practically walking skeletons — and the hot weather has still to come. It was rather terrifying. In India you may travel for days over these great plains, no hills or mountains in sight and only the near horizon of grey-brown earth and sultry sky for hundreds of miles. When we came to the Mahratta country (which we are in now) the mountain ranges showed high in the far distance, getting nearer with more detail and deep gorges. They are all brown and stony, not unlike Baluchistan except there the mountains are pinker and seem to be made of clay. Opposite me now and around the whole saucer of the valley where this camp is, are knife-edged giants as far as the eye can see and only the valley faintly green and speckled with red-flowered trees; and on the highest peak there is a castle-fort built by the Mahratta chieftain Shivaji, called by his followers 'the Mountain Rat' — Heaven knows how he built it or anyone else stormed it.

It will be odd to see green spacious English mountains again after all these years of menacing ranges scattered over India; and to think I once thought that Wastwater was depressing and harsh! The only thing that is ever 'real' is England's Green and Pleasant Land.

Calcutta, 1946

I wonder if you have seen the news of the uprising in the Punjab and the burning of Lahore city, Amritsar city, Taxila and even the delightful hill station of Murree? IT HAS STARTED. Yesterday's paper gave descriptions of the utter slaughter in Amritsar. It is frightful to contemplate, and sounds as bad as the Calcutta killing of last August. The Sikhs are a warlike caste and so are the Muslims and they have been going at each other with knives and swords for four days in the small town of Amritsar. There all the bazaar streets, so narrow and ancient that they scarcely allow two vehicles to pass, radiate like spokes from the hub which is the Golden Temple. The houses are tall with balcony upon balcony, all wood, some beautifully carved and coloured and all complete death traps. The water is nil except around the lake of the Temple and when the Fire Brigade did get through to some of the fires, where really nobody can have had a chance of escape, the mob cut the hoses and fought the firemen — it all sounds too grim for anything. In Lahore, not so far away, the same thing happened — there also the bazaar is intersected with hundreds of tiny alley-streets, each one a death-trap. The merchants are incredibly rich and store most priceless silks and saris in these tiny slits of shops and we read that hundreds have been burnt and the owners with them. The police and troops withheld their fire for nearly two days, trying to calm things but after that the Army came in with full force, firing on mobs, patrolling the streets with tanks and imposing 24-hour curfews and now things are a little better. The Inniskillings and the Yorks and Lancs have marched into Amritsar, where fifty thousand women and children were trying to shelter near the Temple. Rawalpindi starts as the others calm down. Jullundur, a great Sikh stronghold is also up.

In the meantime, we have been watching Calcutta celebrate Holi, the Festival of Spring — if I hadn't had 'flu we should have been in Benares for it, but we shall do Benares next weekend instead.

Holi

Holi is a Hindu festival and the main ritual seems to be in squirting red and purple dye over everyone else's white shirt! There is also a glowing crimson powder, and a fierce green and purple one, which the men rub over their hair and faces and really become the most revolting sights possible. The day is a whole holiday for everyone and we were awakened at a very early hour with buses honking up and down Chowringhee carrying cheering laughing mobs, all in shirts covered with red dye. This went on all day, even most respectable-looking men in new shiny cars quite covered in crimson powder and dye. In a Hindu state, such as Jodhpur, the lower castes who keep the Holi festival are given complete 'fools' licence' for the day and the Maharaja himself must submit to being splashed and dyed if he meets a mob of merrymakers — rather a nice idea once a year! I remember in Hyderabad, Sind, the first year we were there, being invited by the sepoys to see some Holi dancing in the evening at their barracks. As the other wives didn't go (beneath their Army dignity, I discovered afterwards) I was the only European woman there. We were given a most amazing rice and curry supper, I seated on an almost throne-like armchair and Geoffrey and the other officers around. Behind me stood a servant with an enormous peacock-feather fan on a long pole which he waved over me the whole evening to keep me cool. The main show was the nautch, but not done by women — some of the very young sepoys were dressed up in veils and saris and clanking anklets and did the most twisting, writhing and seductive dances possible; their faces were made up like a nautch-dancer's and their long black eyes were outlined with kohl and they really were superb. I remember one of them, looking most realistic, insisted upon vamping Geoffrey, and he descended from our dais and pursued 'her', much to everyone's joy! Then we were all given vast handfuls of sweets and nuts and fruit and garlanded and we went home in the early hours of the morning. When I told the pukka mem-sahibs that I had been to the party they were distinctly uppish. I showed them the sketches I had made too. Really, those Army wives in Hyderabad and four others *didn't* like me much — they had been Army since they were practically schoolgirls and were then very important, their husbands having risen to Majors and Colonels: Geoffrey was only a Lieut. and they all thought us too free and easy. Anyway, that was the merriest Holi I have seen. Here in Calcutta it just seemed to be yelling mobs on buses and in cars.

Calcutta

We leave Calcutta next Tuesday the 3rd December and don't intend to return until mid-January. Geoffrey very conveniently has some Factory inspection to do, and the Army owes us twenty-eight days' leave and so by combining the two and getting a great deal of free travelling, owing to Army warrants, Travel Allowance and the like we have planned a most lovely tour — all, I may say, being started by

Rath, near Fatehpur Sikri.

my saying that the *only* place I wanted to see at Christmas was the Khyber! I always feel that I know every stick and stone of it — and Peshawar has a magic sound. Our hotel is already booked there for December 23rd till the end of the month and I feel so excited. This is our tour programme ...

First to Lucknow. The Prime Minister has sent a wire to G. asking him to come and we feel that the job of Chief Engineer to Cawnpore is again on the tapis — the last time G. went there he had an interview with the charming Mrs. Pundit and her brother, the close-eyed Nehru, and *still* they got no 'Forrarder'. Perhaps this time something will be really settled. G. has been telling them that he is planning to go home in March and doesn't want the job particularly.

From Lucknow we go on to Agra, as G. hasn't seen the Taj, tho' I have when passing thro' in 1940. I saw it both by moonlight and sunrise and it was very lovely. I shall be able to appreciate it more now as I know India better and realise what a dearth of good architecture there is — in fact the Taj is one of three only, judged by British or Continental standards. Then I was fresh from home and not so impressed as I shall be after seven years. From there we go to nearby Fatehpur Sikri and hope to spend a night amidst its ruins and ghosts in company with our friend Sir Walter Gurner, who is an antiquarian by inclination and I.C.S. and key-man in Calcutta by profession. He has asked for the loan of the Archaeological Bungalow on the Site for a night, so it will be doubly interesting. From there to Delhi for a night or so and then Muradnagar, then Rampur where the hounds that are like woolly greyhounds hail from, and then to Amritsar with its Golden Temple, the Holy city of the Sikhs — we have been there once or twice before and never fail to find it tranquil and charming. The Golden Temple stands in the centre of a small lake and weeping willows hung with garlands of yellow flowers droop from the white marble walk around it — then to Lahore where we may probably stay with the Bishop and anyway I like Lahore, the Sikhs wear such wonderful turbans of delicate fondant tints and parade in beautifully cut European trousers which show their narrow hips to perfection; the women usually wear the Punjabi full trousers and almost knee-length satin jumpers, also very waisted and have a contrasting piece of georgette scarf over their shining black plaits — also it is a nice city with lots of parks and trees.

From there we go up to Peshawar which is new ground for us both and then the Khyber which is only about twenty miles away; and thence to the Swat valley and Mardan, Malakand and Dargai — and if you want to know where that is, you will find it in Kipling's poem of East is East. At Mardan there is the Guides' Cavalry chapel which is famous too — then we should go back to Nowshera and to Taxila where we hope to find some remains of Alexander and his Greeks. I have seen some very delightful sculptures carved 800 years after Alexander which show an unmistakably Greek influence still and now we shall see some more I hope — you may remember that in the Lahore Museum Kim saw some of these? After that we may return to Calcutta or we may

A jirgha at Peshawar.

continue to Udaipur and Jaipur; both dreams of a past India set in lakes and steeped in romances of jewels and fair women of long ago — anyway, Delhi for a second visit on our way back. I do look forward to seeing it again too, as when I was there in 1940 I disliked Lutyens' work very much then — so hard and red and unsympathetic to India.

As I write this, after dinner, Geoffrey is reading me bits from the delightful Emily Eden book, Lahore and La Martiniere — the prison full of Thugs (for a *most* interesting book on them, read Sleeman's 'Thugee', an absolutely unbelievable occupation of a death-dealing caste under the patronage of Culcatta's own goddess Kali the Destroyer. She has an evil black face and her tongue is out licking up the blood of her victims — her neck is hung with a circle of human skulls and her hands drip blood — *no wonder* Bengalees are always killing each other! On the banks of the Hooghly here there is a charming little garden named the Eden Garden, after the aforesaid Emily and there is a small stream winding thro' it like a miniature Surpentine and the water buffaloes submerge themselves entirely and lie in the mudge on the bottom, happily blowing bubbles. Water buffaloes are quite hideous anyway — even their calves are and I can think of no other young animals which haven't *some* charm if only just because of their youngness, but the water buffalo is hideous and ungainly from it's birth, poor thing. In the Eden Garden there is also a Burmese pagoda set up with all it's tinkling bells and many roofs on the side of the water and farther on among the trees are clumps of thick-leafed cactus where the young Indians scratch the names of their lady-loves and watch the marks deepen and expand as the leaves grow longer and fleshier — an amusing place, where from the eighteenth century polite Calcutta used to meet and listen to the band on cool evenings, but now nearly deserted.

This morning, in the midst of my packing and sorting of our clothes and possessions for storage, *what* did I do? Sit down and make a poor little sick money a coat of grey flannel! The 'monkey-men' drag these unfortunate little animals about on the end of chains and rattle a drum for them to dance and perform to and the poor things' sad faces are truly depressing. I always gave the animals fruit and milk or water to drink and firmly said 'No tricks'. Last week the man begged for something to make the bigger monkey a coat as it was cold in the mornings and evenings and so I gave him a piece of pink woollen material but so far no coat and the monkey has a bad cough and shivering, so I sat on the grass with it huddled up on my knee and made it a warm coat there and then — but I think it will die and perhaps it is as well; the *only* happy animals in India are the dead ones.

Since telling you about the Great Calcutta Killing, there have been two more whopping orgies, one in the swamp districts of Neokhali and the other in the State of Bihar, the latter exceeding the killings here by literally thousands — complete villages were wiped out, this time by the Hindus who said they were avenging Neokhali and Calcutta, and this town is over-run with refugees who come to the Government camps for food and clothing. It is most terrible to think of, masses of Muslim women were found in wells; they had jumped in at the command of their men-folk and then had stones thrown upon them to hasten death, rather than be 'defiled' by infidels — think of it — and all the males, both grown up and babies, were put to the knife and sword. Calcutta still has a rigid 10.30 p.m. to 5 a.m. curfew and the armed guards and tanks go rumbling down the main roads every night, otherwise we should have no peace at all — *and*, I may add, the peace is being kept by British troops; of course!

Agra

We were in Agra at the beginning of the week — the moon was at its brightest and we are still bemused with the beauty of the Mogul Taj. The whole building seemed to swim in silver vapour, its sheen like a grey pearl, glowing where the moonlight touched it — I had forgotten that it was so beautiful. I first saw it in 1940 during my first few months in the country and then felt slightly disappointed because the whole building and its long water gardens were so exactly like the photographs that nothing was left to the imagination this time but the sheer *magic* and unsurpassed beauty of white

Mosque at Agra.

marble, soft as old ivory seen against bright stars and soft blue night, were completely overwhelming. We went into the tomb, and were again astounded by the exquisite workmanship of the inlaid agate, black marble, cornelian and other stones, which had a Biblican sound as the Guide said their names over.

We took a car and motored twenty-five miles out to Akbar's deserted city of Fatehpur Sikri, spending a whole day with a charming old guide, who only told us what we wanted to know, and had no 'set piece'. He was a descendent of the saint whose marble tomb stands in the centre courtyard of the great mosque and the guide's later ancestors are all buried near by and he showed us where his own tomb would be placed. The famous 'divers' did their leap from a battlemented wall into a walled well below, green and stinking — 100 feet in all — they *jump* — and land feet first. Apart from this saint's little mosque-like tomb, all the other buildings are of old pinky-red sandstone, most beautifully carved. We were struck with the restraint and consequent perfection of all the carving, a single line being enough in some cases and in others intricate twining and foliage, and remembered some of the Hindu horrors that we have seen lately, also carved and ornamented in the name of religion, but of such a clutter, figure upon figure, more than half obscene to our minds and, in the mass, forming nothing of a design or balance at all. So, in the two religions, Mussulman is almost Puritanical in his outlook, strict and unbending in his beliefs, while the Hindu has such a clutter of gods of every kind, including the monkey and the cow and all its excretia into the bargain.

The Red Fort of the Moguls in Delhi was another joy to us, again giving a perfection of line and plan, both of the water-gardens and the buildings. The marble palace where once stood the Peacock Throne had us enthralled for nearly an hour: the inlay and paintings and purity of the marble grilles must have been quite glorious when the Mogul Emperors lived there. Lord Curzon (as usual!) had restored a great deal of it, and brought back some of the inlay that had been stolen or sold. Wherever one goes in India, it is always Lord Curzon who has been instrumental in restoring the past glories and I don't think people realise what they owe to him.

Riaz Ahamed; guide at Fatehpur Sikri.

Cawnpore

As my travellings seem to amuse you and not bore you, shall I tell you about our latest 'tour' to Cawnpore of Massacre fame?

Geoffrey had always told me of the lovely Club at Cawnpore and it *is* nice and has an open air and very modern swimming-pool under the trees on the lawn. The original club was started about 1812 as a mere library for the young subalterns. An earnest and good-minded lady was shocked at their carry-ons and

Massacre Ghat, Cawnpore.

tipsy orgies and felt it was up to her to start a rest-room and library so that they should have something other than women and drink to occupy their youthful minds. This room is now the lounge and the rest of the club has gradually been built around it and has a nice ballroom too and married quarters for residents; you'll see why I'm emphasisng this, later. The rest of the Cantonment is typical of all the British Cantonments in India, rather dry and dusty with nice colour-washed bungalows and compounds with shady trees and tree bordered roads — rather flat and extremely *hot* and dusty up to June, when the rains break and then a welter of green they say and a very cold winter to balance the scorching summer. Two weeks ago, when we were there, it was much hotter and drier than Calcutta, which was pretty unbearable.

    Behind the Cantonment flows the sacred Ganges. The river-bed is immensely broad but the river a small trickle over mud flats at the moment and along the banks are the gardens of the

Massacre Ghat — new bungalows — that is, built after 1857 when the original ones were burnt and razed to the ground and have their gardens to the river's edge. One or two have small swimming-pools under the trees that must have been there before the Mutiny and there are old wells with the bullock-slope still shiny from use. It is still a commonplace sight to see the two white bullocks pulling the mussac or skin from the well as they rush down the fifty yard slope. A man at the top hauls the mussac over the well's edge and the water is spilled into a runnel which waters the garden or field. The fact that half the water is wasted by being spilled back over the well's edge is too elementary a fact to be noticed in this country.

Through some iron gates is a broad path leading to a Hindu temple, a Mussulman masjid and a pathetic and lonely Christian cross on the side of the ghat. When the river is full the waters come up to the foot of the cross. Twisted in and out of the two small buildings is the most amazing and ancient-looking banyan-tree — some of its limbs have the white walls built around and under them. This is the place where all the women and children who had been granted 'safe-conduct' across the river in 1857 were suddenly set upon, fired upon and murdered by the natives. There is a real feeling of Doom and Woe and Horror to this very day and the tree that must have been there then is still there, vast and still. I sat and sketched it and the tree memorials and felt a tension as tho' it might just have happened or would be happening at any moment.

Not very far away is a small park carefully tended by malis and a ticket must be bought at the gate from a guard. Up till recently NO INDIAN was allowed in at all, it is British Govt. property anyway, but now they may come in but not into the little graveyard which is surrounded by iron trellis covered with yellow tea-roses. Here are the remains of more bungalows — just a few stones here and there and a very ornate and undoubtedly Ruskin-inspired Gothic monument on a small hill. Inside it is the well, now sealed and richly ornamented and resembling a font. Here the bodies of the living and dead were hurled by the Mutineers, after they had been hacked to pieces by the town butchers. The native sepoys refused to kill women and children in cold blood, tho' they had fired on them and besieged the bungalows for weeks and so when the British Army was nearing and they knew they would be beaten, the Nana Sahib had the women and children imprisoned in the cellars and the men of the butcher caste to hack them up and throw them into the well. This old part of Cawnpore screams with history of the British during the Mutiny and it is only when one is really on the spot that the whole episode becomes real. As Geoffrey says, these monuments, beautifully carved and brought out stone by stone from England, represent far more money than it would have taken to make the place *safe* in 1856-7 and the whole ghastly affair need never have happened. I was glad to leave and try and shake off the grim fear that everything reeked of.

The new part of Cawnpore is a good way away from all this and mainly mills. Imagine Manchester or Widnes set in narrow tree-edged lanes with blue sky overhead and perpetual sunshine and you have it. Some of the oldest mills in India are here — the Elgin Mills started just after the Mutiny f'rinstance — most of the sheets and towels and lining things one ever buys are made here — carpets — big hide tanneries — chemical works. The United Provinces have conspired to turn the city into a congested and hideous place, filled with slums and narrow roads and around the edge are dotted the wealthy European Box-wallah's new bungalows. There is a big Scotch colony, jute, as here in Calcutta and just as jungli and crude no doubt. Immense wealth everywhere we were told.

When Geoffrey had finished the inspection of Factories for H.M.G. — the job which brought us to Cawnpore — we left the Inspection Bungalow in the Cantonment, where I had spent the first three days in bed (*wot* a bed!) with a slight attack of pleurisy; the second time I've had it after travelling in an Indian train. The latter have to be completely shut up at night as train thieves and murders seem to be the order of the day, or night, now. Then when all shutters have been put up and locked there is, of course, very little if any air, so the fan has to be on all night. The bunks are narrow and slippery and one's bedclothes come off and then the fan plays a draught on one's chest and lungs. Geoffrey got the Staff Surgeon for me, as I was feeling the worse for wear and he, wretched man, kept me in bed for three days with all kinds of things to drink and breathe — *very* trying. Anyway, as soon as all this was better I got up and went one morning with Geoffrey to help inspect the *vast* munition factory, covering acres of land, which was put up in a hurry in 1942-3 and which will now have to be switched to making something peaceful if possible.

Then we went to stay with a very nice Scot, Sir Edward Souter, who has lived in Cawnpore for about thirty-three years and made a fortune there out of bricks and mortar. He is the guiding light of the Cawnpore Improvement Trust and appears to have the semi-Indian Committee in the palm of his hand. These industrialists, having made the most appalling mess of a once pleasant spot, now have this newly-formed Improvement Scheme to clear it up again. They, or at least Sir Edward, wrote to Geoffrey some months ago and offered him the job of re-planning the city and surrounding countryside, but we felt that if there were anything else in the world to do we'd rather not live in Cawnpore. So Geoffrey told them that. They countered by doubling the offered salary and making any and every concession he named, so that in the end he thought he might as well go and at least see Sir Edward, the world being what it is. Anyway it is the kind of job that a Town Planner and Architect would dream of, given a better climate. While we were there we were still thinking 'God forbid', better stay in the Army another year or go home and do a year's research (G. has just sold a couple of houses at home and planned to use some of the cash as a year's salary), but now we have almost decided to take the Cawnpore job and today G. was to send Sir E. a wire to say he'd take it — the DIE IS CAST. He is not home yet so I don't know the latest — tell you later.

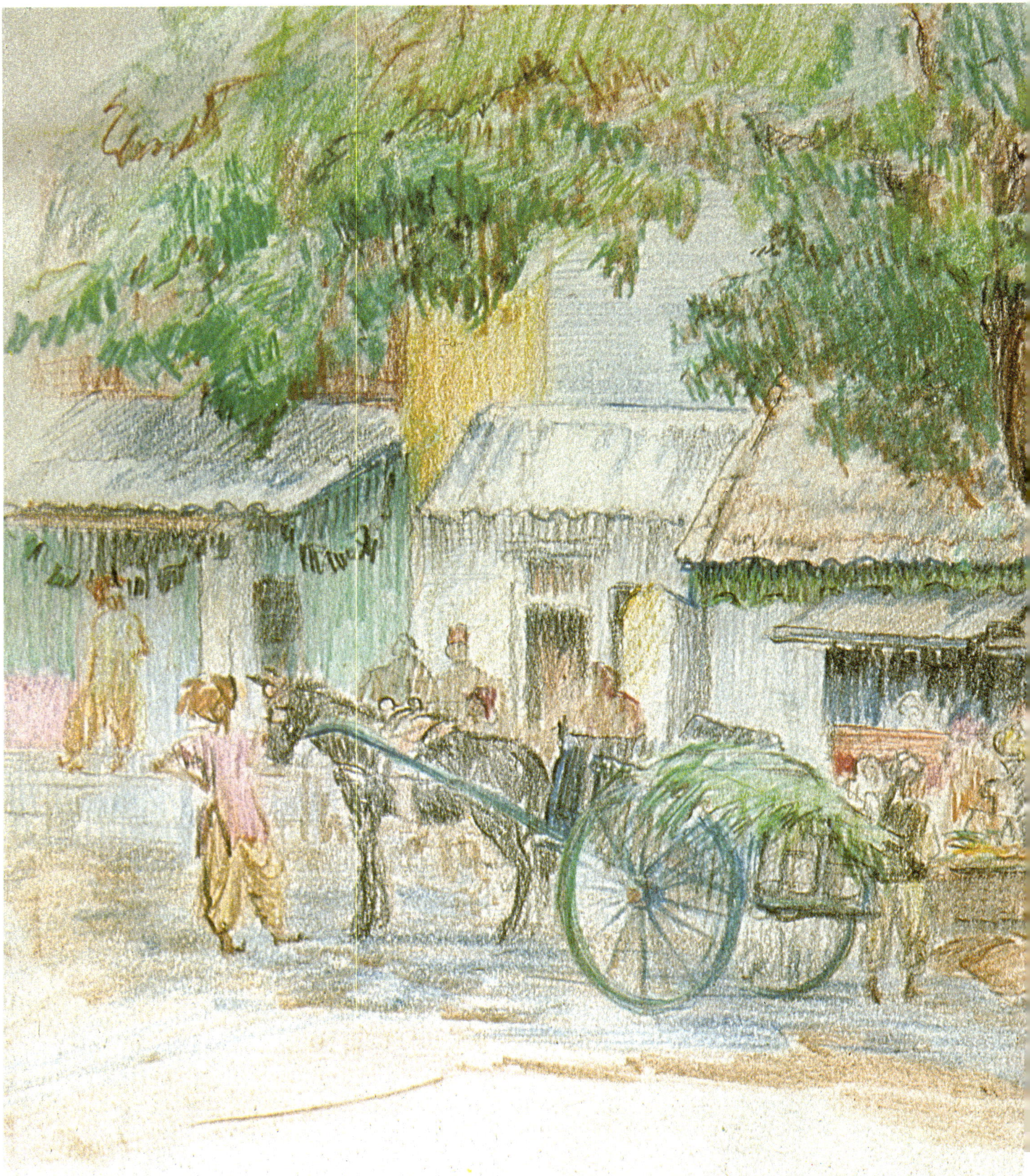

Village scene.

The Residency, Lucknow.

Lucknow

Lucknow is the capital of the U.P. and the usual charming residential town next door to the commercial city. It really *is* a delightful spot and compares very favourably with Delhi — in fact from what I can remember of the latter, Lucknow has it every time. We were lucky to have an Army car, a station-wagon affair, and petrol for fifty miles. It was the first time that Geoffrey and I had travelled by car in India and we loved it all. The way to Lucknow — Nucklow as all Indians call it, the uneducated Class I mean — is thro' fields of barleys and rye and cotton. The few tiny villages we saw seemed amazingly clean and tidy — so few places in this country are clean that one forgets what it looks like! The streets are wide and clean and shady, the buildings are well designed and imposing and well spaced and there is an easy air of gracious well being — now, if we were destined to live *there*; but of course there is no need for improvement there! The United Services Club is an old Mohammedan palace. The very distinctive arches and domed ceilings remain unaltered so that there are rooms through rooms, painted white with the frailest line design of dark blue all over the domed ceilings and down the outline of the arches. Looks as tho' someone had traced it with a feather — rather fascinating! The whole building faces onto the river and was at one time the home of thirty queens, each having her own suite.

Our first essaye was to the Residency, of course! It is just outside the town and not one building, as most Residencies are, but a collection of houses, now ruins, the Residency itself in the centre of them all and the whole park entered by huge stone arches and a gate. Everything is beautifully kept by a posse of malis and hundreds of monkeys leap about in the big trees.

The Curator, who has an office in the Residency, told us that his grandfather was in the Siege. The rooms are covered with old prints which give an idea of the place before the bombardment, during it and the final rescue by General Havelock — most interesting. I sat out in the grounds making as many sketches as I could, especially of the blackened and ruined tower topped by the British flag. Lord Curzon, who did so much for India in preserving old monuments and customs, arranged that there should be a new flag hoisted in the dead of night every three months, so that it appears to be everlasting. One was not conscious of any of the feeling of horror and misery that pervaded Cawnpore, tho' there were some terrible things done in Lucknow in 1857 too. We went to a great walled garden, guarded by strong elephant gates, which was the last stronghold of the Mutineers. Here the Highlanders who had done a forced march from Cawnpore with Havelock made a breech and poured in, killing literally thousands of the native Mutineers to the war-cry of 'Cawnpore, Cawnpore'. Many had found their wives and little children mangled corpses in the cellars or down the well and so not a native was spared — and I think our losses were just about fifty men.

On the other side of the lake, where the buffaloes were wallowing, is the ruined shell of Dilkusha, a lovely name, meaning the Happy Heart. Its towers were used as lookout posts by the British. When it was still the Happy Heart the last King of Oudh lived there, a dissipated but cheerful fat man, and the most powerful man in his kingdom was his English barber who had started life as a cabin-boy and who eventually ran the palace and all that it contained. Needless to add he retired a very rich man and became an M.P.! Dilkusha was designed by an Italian and the few broken and bullet-scarred columns that remain at the top of a grand flight of steps are still lovely. We got up early on our last morning and took a pony-trap out there so that I might make some sketches and then G. took snapshots of it and La Martiniere and we pelted back to pack and catch the train for Calcutta.

The 'Happy Heart', Dilkusha.

*The Palace, Rampur
December 13th, 1946*

We were in Delhi for the past three days and I did a small amount of sketching while Geoffrey buzzed around doing his job. Our train from Delhi to here left at 4 a.m. and we were rather worried about getting a taxi at that hour from Maidens Hotel to the station, so Geoffrey booked a Rest Room in the station of which there are six and we had all our things put in there and after dinner we went to bed; could have had a bath but didn't and generally made ourselves comfortable until a chokidar called us at 3 a.m. with some very Indian home-brewed tea and shaving-water! Then all we had to do was to stir up a few coolies and go along to our platform where the Rampur train was, make up our beds in the coupé and go to sleep again.

This is a Christmas letter and I thought you would like to have it on Palace writing-paper! We only arrived a few hours ago, I not knowing in the least that we were to be the Nawab's guests but apparently Geoffrey did and kept it up his sleeve as a surprise for me. I *like* palaces and this is a particularly superb one with the most lovely architecture of tall columns and arches looking onto smooth lawns and marble fountains, with groves of feathery eucalyptus-trees carefully planted in careless symmetry. Some European landscape-gardener must have done it all, as it is exceptionally charming. Around the broad main drive are globes of subdued light instead of ordinary lamps and there is a bright gleam on the top of the flagpole, which is surmounted by the Nawab's crown. As it is now half-past five and the dusk upon us, somebody has turned all the garden lamps on. Our bedroom suite looks onto the garden thro' Mogul arches and all the floors of the verandas and our rooms are white marble. The rooms are white, with marble mantlepiece and two bathrooms — the great joy of the latter is that there are *hot* towel-rails, so that one is in a nice warm atmosphere because it is *cold* in this part of the world. Living in Calcutta and only touring in Bengal lately, I had forgotten how jolly cold it can be — a good practice for our return home next year.

I must tell you more about our suite, as it is all so simple and charming. The curtains over the doors onto the verandas and which divide the dressing-rooms are of old gold and the blankets on the two very high brass beds are the same colour — the carpet is mainly yellow-gold, with an Indian design in pale blue and the electric-light shades are of most lovely cut glass. When we arrived today after lunch we were brought up here and immediately given coffee, special cigarettes in a silver case, and matches in a box with the 'royal crest'. The silver coffee and milk-pots were of an elegant Regency design on a plain silver tray. You cannot realise how *very* civilised this all seems to us, as the average Indian, however rich, invariably goes in for a vast amount of tiddly-widdly decoration and as likely as not the tea or coffee-pot will be in the shape of an aeroplane of the Wright Bros. period, or an old motor car or train! Things are usually terribly and fearfully ornate, but in fairness to all I must own that these have belonged to Hindus and our host here is a Mohammedan, and their culture is much more restrained.

Downstairs are huge reception rooms, one with a modified throne under a canopy, which is obviously for State occasions — really lovely glass chandeliers hang down the centre and discreetly between the white and gold and turquoise columns at the sides of the room hang fans because it is exceedingly hot here in the summertime. There is a ballroom with all the oddments of a modern dance band on a platform at one end, this room which looks out onto a long terrace is the least good of any, as it is in rather an 'early Corner House' style but the dance floor would take hundreds and looks most inviting. Here all the carpets flanking the sides are mauve and the damask upholstery is almost purple on jade green wood. The dining-room which runs at right angles has a yellowish-brown glass chandelier over the table — I've not seen that coloured glass before — and the wall brackets are of the same glass and the chairs all have two hungry open-mouthed lions on the backs. I also saw a sweet little sitting-room in powder blue and grey damask and another drawing-room with a grand piano, mainly rich red satin damask and a lot of carved wood and some *vast* pictures, one of Kanchenjunga in the sunset, done by an Indian. You will see that I did a great deal of looking around!

     We were also very interested in the masses of old knives, talwars (curved swords), pistols and antique guns that are arranged on boards reaching the ceiling, in the hall and up the main stairway. We have seen the same sort of thing in Jodhpur, in the Fort Museum, but not just loose about the house, so to speak. At the moment the Nawab is at the Fort, but I have given my best evening gown to the dhobi to be pressed, in view of tonight's dinner — *pause,* while I receive a mass of roses which are grown outside near the big fountain. They are beauties, pink and white and one or two deep red — I really *am* enjoying myself!

Today we have visited the Fort, in which is another palace — the Nawab's Winter Palace. His father was a great traveller and went

State bedroom, Rampur Fort.

Cut-glass furniture.

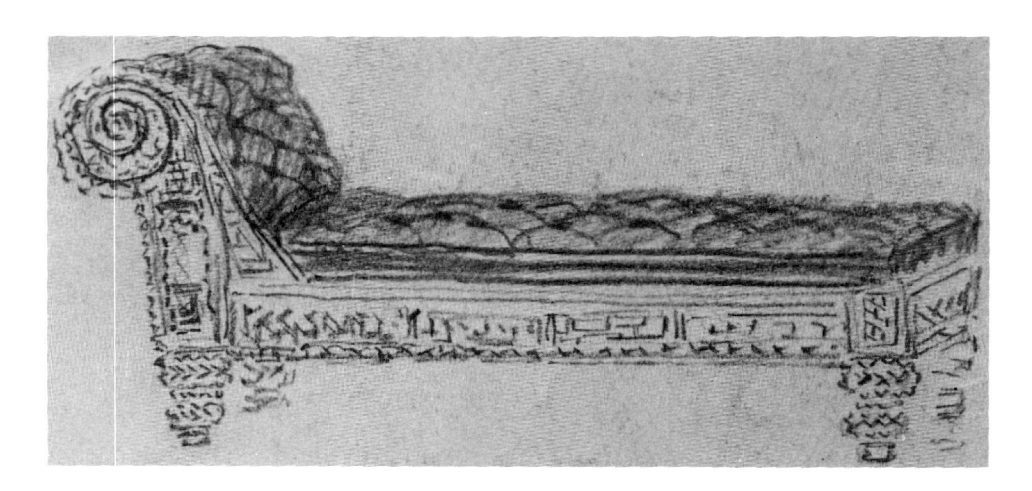

shopping all over Europe with the wealth of India in his pockets, so that now the great domes and arched Guest House is a museum for his treasures. He brought many pictures and bronzes from Paris and every room, both down and upstairs, is filled to overflowing with later Victorian beauties, huge nudes from the Paris schools and marble and silver statues. There was one small figure of François I on horseback which was of pure silver and most striking — around the great hall under the dome there are full-sized marbles of coy ladies sitting or rising from their baths and on the walls almost life-sized paintings of tigers in the death grip of a python and, to balance it, a charging rhino of ferocious aspect. Some of the furniture in the drawing and dining-rooms seems fantastic to our Western eyes, a whole suite of CUT GLASS upholstered in deep purple plush was perhaps the most striking — the sofa, chairs and footstool gleamed in the late afternoon sunshine as the padded covers were removed for us. In another room was a complete sideboard — chiffonier the Victorians called it, I think — of solid hallmarked English silver, the various recesses backed with mirror and housing priceless enamel vases. Cut glass and silver chandeliers and table lamps and tables were everywhere and the walls laden with big, small and indifferent oil paintings.

But even all this was eclipsed by the State bedroom up stairs. Here every single article of furniture was of pure silver, the chairs and divans and sofas upholstered in magenta velvet, and in the centre stood a double bed that only Hollywood could have imagined and brought to life. It was a dream of delicate workmanship, the four posts supporting a silver frame overhead for a pink pleated-satin dome, surmounted with a large silver crown. On all the four sides were the frailest silk net curtains, sprinkled with silver sequins and beads and inside the lace and embroidered silk coverings looked like gossamer. At the foot was a low and broad couch, the frame of silver and the sausage-shaped pillow and satin covering of pink covered with embroidered muslin. At the foot of this, on the floor, was a Persian carpet with more cushions for reclining and resting, and nearby was a chaise longue of silver and magenta velvet — and around and about more silver armchairs, tables, statues and vases. The panelled walls were of turquoise blue and gold and the ceiling gold and white squared. Over the white marble mantlepiece was one of the most lovely paintings I have ever seen of a sleeping woman. She lay amidst satin and chiffons, pale as her skin and her body half-covered with turquoise taffeta and sky blue satin draperies. In her hand was a blue fan and behind her draperies of blond satin faintly embroidered. The light fell across her closed eyes and mouth and across her creamy white bosom and bare arms and across the right hand corner was a brilliant touch of cardinal-red satin curtain. The whole was in full keeping with the exotic room — needless to add, the artist was a Frenchman.

Lahore

Punjabi bullock cart

Then to Lahore, where the Christmas Race Week visitors filled every hotel, and we were lucky to get rooms at all. It all felt very festive and we did quite a lot of shopping and I managed to find some drawing pencils and inks — wonderful! As in Delhi, the little two-wheeled tongas were everywhere and we practically 'bought' one for the time we were there, the same man coming every morning. He had a very beautiful and high-spirited pure white pony which was dressed in the most costly harness and silver collar, plumes and bells, and which was the pride and joy of his life. They all love horses, these Punjabi men and the country around is noted for its fine animals. This driver wouldn't have an Indian fare — he was only for Sahibs he said — and he couldn't really believe that we were all going to leave the country. He begged Geoffrey to take him to England as a syce, when we go. We made a state call on the Bishop and he and his wife and her sister were most kind. They all knew G's father and mother when G. was a small boy. The Bishop is a most magnificent specimen of a man and was obviously destined to be a Bishop from his earliest curacy!

      On December 22nd there was to be a carol service in the Cathedral and so we packed everything for the station and left it ready, got into our lovely white pony tonga and rushed along to the Cathedral for 6.30 and sang lustily. It was a most charming service, the choir giving various carols alone and between each a few verses from the Bible were read, starting with the smallest black-faced choirboy, then lay reader, then a deaconess, and so on, until the last one, before the last carol, was read by the Lord Bishop himself, resplendent in his red and purple. We then rushed out to the tonga and tore along to the station in time for the train.

Peshawar

A corner of Peshawar.

Peshawar city.

Then, by the Night Frontier Mail, ablaze with the vast searchlight that every Indian train has on its head, to the North-West Frontier Province and our real holiday started, Peshawar, and 'Christmas in the Khyber' having been our watchword. The Vale of Peshawar is quite the most fertile valley imaginable and between the bright green rows of winter wheat were lines of fruit trees, leafless and bare, making a beautiful tracery against the far distant blue ranges that surround the plain like the rim of a bowl. The air was cold but a pale sun shone all day and we were quite thrilled to feel chilly in the mornings and have to wait for the bedroom fire to be lighted before we put our toes out of bed! We met quite a lot of friends and had much jollity, such as the Hunt Ball of the famous Peshawar Vale Hunt dances, dining at Government House and so forth.

Then with great luck *and* luxury we hired a car for a week and started to tour the Khyber. The twisting tortuous road up the pass to the Afghan border is just as grimly fascinating as one always imagines it. Everywhere are dotted small picket towers, the entrance near to the top and the ladder withdrawn inside by the guard. The towers may belong to some tribe or they may be picketed by men of the Khyber Rifles, but they are grimly useful and no man or boy is ever seen anywhere, even in the main bazaar of Peshawar City, without a rifle on his shoulder and bristling cartridge belt at his waist. The O.C. Khyber Rifles, Col. Booth, who lives at the top of the Pass at Landi Kotal in the Cantonment and Fort overlooking the wild ranges of Afghanistan, asked us to lunch with him and then took us even farther afield. He was interested in my sketching and he made plans for the next day, when I was to review the Pathans of both Jamrud and Shagai Forts with him and pick out the men I wanted for models! Can you imagine what a thrill it was for me? Or me, next day, in a bitter howling wind, walking up and down the ranks with him, saying 'I'll have him, and him,' and I really chose some devastating types, with the grim Afridi look that is so typical — light skins and most usually rather amber coloured eyes and black hair and beaky noses. They were all very vain, these ruffians, and *loved* being sketched!

On guard, Landi Kotal.

Fortified house.

Men of the Khyber Rifles.

Political Agent's bungalow, Malakand.

After the New Year we decided it was time to move on, and so took the car and driver and set out for Malakand. On the way we passed through Mardan, where the Guides' Cavalry used to be stationed. There is the famous Guides' Chapel there, quite a tiny place, but the walls are covered in brass tablets in memory of the many famous men who have given their lives to keeping the peace on the Frontier. In the small churchyard there were many graves, the General and other officers on one side and the Other Ranks on t'other — even in death they were orderly, it seemed!

Malakand and Swat

Then we left the valley and started to wind up and up and up, on a perilously twisting but well kept road, until we reached Malakand. The Governor had invited us to stay in the Circuit House, which is within the walls of the Fort, manned by an Assamese regiment with

Malakand.

British Officers. The fort is built on the tip-top crag of one of the rocky foothills — most fascinating place, most unreal and remote.

After a few days of sketching and motoring, we packed up again and went on to the Swat Valley — a lovely place that reminded me of the Lake District on a misty day. The Kabul river came, icy and green, leaping over boulders and across the valley. The countryside was grey-green and tawny and apart from the casuarina-trees that lined all the roads, the trees were leafless and bare with a few yellow berries here and there — quite lovely. The only leaves were in the dark green orange groves, which covered the ground for miles. All the smaller trees were wrapped up in straw like haystacks, to protect them from the winter's cold. On the bigger ones oranges were still hanging.

The Ruler of Swat is called the Wali, as you may know from your Lear. He is a Muslim, loves the British (we made his family the rulers) and has an ever-ready suite in his Guest House awaiting visitors. Guards telephoned up the valley as our car passed and so when we reached the Palace there was a complete reception committee on the doorstep awaiting us and we found we were expected to stay a few days. Unfortunately we could not but I should have loved to have done so. The Palace and Mosques with white domes and minarettes against the towering snow-covered mountains

Chakdara Fort, Swat Valley.

Hassan-Abdul from the Dak bungalow.

Hassan-Abdul at sunset.

seemed like a forgotten Paradise — a Shangri-la. But we had tea and lots of talk.

Then back down the Pass in our large yellow car, staying the night at a tiny old-fashioned Dak bungalow at Hassan-Abdul, on the fork of the Abbottabad-Rawalpindi road. It was most antiquated, minus any electric lighting but we had the most enormous wood fire made in the big bedroom (no real bed, only charpoys) and with an oil lamp dotted here and there we did very nicely, having our meals on a table by the blazing fire. In the room was the wooden frame of an antique hand-punka, worked by a rope threaded thro' a hole in the door frame and pulled (in hot weather) by a punka-boy sitting on the veranda. These old things are usually better at giving a good draught of air thro' the room than the modern electric fan but the snag of course is that the boy, having tied the rope to his big toe, goes to sleep! I was so enthralled with this relic of old India that I made a sketch of it all.

Taxila

We wanted to go to Taxila, the ancient city that was founded by Alexander, which is just up the Valley. The place itself is just a 'dig' and not really very interesting apart from the manner in which the dry stone walls were laid. It ranks with Mahenjo Daro, in the Indus valley, as one of the earliest known civilisations with main drainage complete and more than one has these days in most Cantonments! All the lovely statuary, heads, jewellery, etc., are housed in a new nearby museum, all most interesting — Buddhist-gone-Greek, with a freedom of carving and moulding that is quite unknown in India now-a-days.

The next day we went on to Rawalpindi, passing a huge

Bedroom in the Dak bungalow.

monolith memorial to John Nicholson that guards the narrow pass into the farther valley. In 'Pindi we looked up some old friends and then said goodbye to the car, which went back to Peshawar, while we caught the Delhi train. There we stayed just a day and, as the man Geoffrey had to see was away, we took another train on the narrow Native State Railway to Jaipur.

   The hotel was almost deserted, tho' this, being the cold weather, is the tourist season. People said that the general disturbances and the killing in Calcutta and Bihar had deterred all sorts of people from travelling and all the merchants who usually made fortunes in other years were very down in the mouth. Of course the whole of India suffers from this unrest. In Peshawar we talked with a very wealthy fruit grower whose produce comes down to Calcutta and Bombay. Last August and September he lost literally thousands of pounds (money) on the fruit that rotted in the warehouses and sidings because there were no men to deal with it — all too busy killing or being killed and then afterwards too frightened to work.

Skinner's Mosque, Old Delhi.

Jaipur

The old pink and white 'birthday cake' buildings of Jaipur and the great wide streets were most impressive but, of course, only a façade and at one street deep one gets to all the squalor and filth and misery of any other Indian town. The wide roads lack trees and seem very bleak and the summer there must be utter hell in the heat, as it was dusty enough when we there in January.

We rode on elephants to the hill-top where the sixteenth century Palace of Amber looks over the surrounding countryside, and were fascinated by a serpentine 'great wall' which meandered over hill and dale as a bygone State protection.

Then back to Delhi again as Geoffrey got a bad chill on his lungs (it was cold riding so high on the elephants, I say!) and he had to spend a day or two in bed, a fire in his room, ministered to by the Staff Surgeon. There wasn't even a fireplace in the Jaipur hotel, as they didn't think it was ever really cold. We were frozen and so we fled with rapidity as soon as Geoffrey started to feel really ill, as we didn't want to be stuck in Jaipur for very long.

New Delhi

New Delhi goes on giving me the complete WILLIES — it is quite the most dreary and depressing place possible on a winter afternoon. The huge, new bleak bare buildings that Lutyens built, the Secretariat etc., stand grimly naked. The base and first floor are of red sandstone and the upper part pale grey. The proportions are wrongly coloured to start with, and the long endless avenues radiating therefrom have no curve of interest to take the eye; very few trees, just a line of bright lights coming to a pin-point — traffic also seems a pin-point, as the roads are very wide. Taxis are prohibitive in price and practically *everyone* takes a little two-wheeled tonga drawn by a small pony. The drivers, by some strange intuition that is baffling to a mere visitor, seem to be able to find their way thro' these vastly long vistas where no one walks — no one is seen at all — the houses are so far set in their gardens that no lights are seen and it is like a city of the dead — in fact Akbar's deserted city of Fatehpur Sikri is *full* of vitality compared with New Delhi.

Now we are back in the welcome warmth of Bengal — I never thought I should be glad to see filthy Calcutta again, but we both are.

*St John's Church,
Old Delhi.*

We are living in a suite in the biggest hotel here and our sitting-room and Geoffrey's dressing-room-cum-writing-room look out over the Maidan and its green tree-tops to the Hooghly and the shops and the Fort.

We expect to stay here until the office moves up to Simla about the end of March and there we shall probably live in another hotel until we leave Bombay for HOME. I own that I have loved being in India and have never really had a dull moment for quite seven years but now, when there is so much political upset and turmoil and the uneasy peace only kept by the presence of good British troops armed with guns and tanks and armoured cars, it is high time to leave. There are other countries to visit and I am sure that poor old England, who seems to bear the brunt of all the wars and the Peace, needs people who are willing to work for her. We long for the sight of a British crowd, drab tho' they may be. Anyway, fat Bengalis in dhotis of dirty white are not inspiring.

Kolhapur

I don't think I told you of our last trip to Bombay, Poona and Kolhapur, did I? As there was shooting and knifing and general riot and turmoil in Bombay, we deferred our visit for a week and went to Poona first. Geoffrey had a Munition Factory at Kirkee to look at and spent about two days doing that, while I visited friends. We found that we had a great many in Poona, some from Karachi and some from Quetta and Hyderabad — all I.C.S. or Army. It was grand to see them again and on our last day we gave a big luncheon party at the very nice West of India Club. India really is rather like a great big family house and one is always meeting old friends wherever one goes. Afterwards we did a lovely thing — went to the little native State of Kolhapur by the night train and arrived at the very charming and 'English country-house' Residency for breakfast. Our old friend Colonel Neate lives there with Col. Harvey the Resident and apart from them there are just six other Europeans. The Prime Minister is a delightful I.C.S. man with an American wife and he and Col. Harvey control the State until the real ruler who is only four can take charge! We were shown the Palace by the Indian A.D.C. who lives there with the rather fat but quite young Rani and her little son.

We have seen old old palaces built in Forts, which are more like places in a fairy-tale and we have seen modern and newly built palaces with all Mod. Con. and sophisticated cocktail bars but this Kolhapur palace was about fifty years old and mainly modelled on Balmoral, I should think! It is a Mahratta State and so all the rather bad stained-glass windows in the Durbar hall were depicting the many dubious but valiant episodes in the life of Sivaji, the Mahratta hero. We found that we knew more of the stories than the A.D.C. in the end! At one end of the huge room was a bigger-than-life plaster statue of his fat and late Highness the Rani's husband. He was not the father of the little heir, who was adopted a few weeks before H.H. died in accordance with the Hindu custom so that he should have a 'son' to get him out of the quite inevitable Hell he would be plunged into on his death. The statue was correctly clothed and bedizened and sword-girt but the feet were wearing buttoned BOOTS and both for the left foot — slight mistake somewhere we felt! Upstairs we were shown the little boy's modern nurseries (he was away for a holiday): masses and masses of clockwork toys, wooden toys and motors, carved animals and coloured balls — and dolls.

In the centre of his bedroom was his pale blue spray-painted cot and nearby an almost full-length Chippendale mirror of solid silver! The armchairs and couch were covered in *black* plush (loose covers) and had vast orange cushions all over them — the strangest mixture you ever saw. The rest of the rooms had been modernised for the Rani and the floors covered with most lovely

Window.

pale-coloured carpets of rather nice modern designs — one bit of leafy bamboo across a corner perhaps — and the sofas, which would seat about ten in a row, upholstered in thick peach satin or yellow satin; lots of coloured glass around and a few bowls of tired goldfish.

'Charlie Sahib'

Kolhapur is really famous for two things — its Stud Farm and its hunting Cheetahs. A great Lonsdale-yellow coach — landau is the correct term I think — came for us to take us to the Stud Farm. In the landau sat Charles Cook, known throughout the State as 'Charlie Sahib' to both high and low and he just doesn't remember that he was once Mr. Cook. He is an Australian, as Cockney as you have ever imagined and quite a small man topped with a colossal sombrero. After that, one just has to stop and pause. He is indescribably *battered.* His poor feet just don't seem to belong to him, his chest is the queerest shape as if all the rib bones had been broken and badly set and even his face is odd and his nose broken. Quite literally he has been stamped on and jumped on by wild Australian horses all his life and is now practically a cripple. (G. and I wondered if he can have been a very good horseman!) Anyway, God only knows what his past has been, but at present he is lord of all he surveys in the horse world and is wholly responsible for the Stud Farm of valuable animals and all the racing horses and the buying thereof. He was most amiable to us and Col. Neate and ordered out all the stallions one by one, some most *wild*-looking things, took us to the racing-stable which has 100 stalls and then in the landau, drawn by two great Walers, to the far fields to see the mares and foals and the yearlings. His racy Cockney voice never stopped and really he was extremely knowledgeable and amusing.

Then we went to see the hunting Cheetahs, and the old landau bounced and swayed over the roads like a covered wagon in the films. The people said they would 'lay on' a Cheetah hunt for us in two days time — the animals have to be starved the day before — but we said 'no' to that, and I couldn't bear to think some lovely Black Buck should be pulled down for my benefit, so Charlie Sahib told us how the hunt was conducted. Six Cheetahs and their keepers are taken out in a specially made brake, rather like a jaunting-car, and when the herd of buck is sighted, the beaters send the herd towards the brake. The does go ahead with the fawns and the bucks, who are most inquisitive, stay behind a little. The Cheetahs, who have been hooded like hawks up to now, are half-leashed and in single numbers their hoods are taken off. The first one springs down, takes a second to adjust himself to the light, *sights* and *marks* just one buck out of the running herd and is on him like a flash of light. As soon as he is off the second one is released, and so on. He fells the buck with his hand and then pounces on its throat and just strangles it — no tearing of skin or blood anywhere — and by the time all this has happened the keeper has come up with the hood. The buck's throad is cut and a small quantity of gore is run off into a monster ladle and the Cheetah is allowed to drink, then he is game for another hunt that day — if he eats he won't play any more.

We expected to find these fierce Cheetahs in pens, and I said I hoped there were good iron bars to protect us but we were astonished when we were taken into a big barn affair. Dotted about were large charpoys and on each was a recumbant Cheetah and next to it, curled up amongst the soft fur, was a sleeping syce or keeper! They certainly had nice strong collars and thick chains tied to the charpoy, but apart from that they were lose and so friendly. The syces told us to come and stroke them, so we did and the beautiful things put up their big bullet heads for us to tickle their throats, just like vast tame cats. Then they started to *purr* — and *what* a purring — deep down in their tummies with a rumble that shook! We noticed that they had hands and feet like dogs and not retractable claws like a tiger so that they would naturally fell a buck rather than tear it.

Poona and Bombay

Our last adventure was when we returned on the small branch railway from Kolhapur to Poona on the Sunday evening. It is so small that there are no 1st class coaches and even the Resident has to emerge from a 2nd class or has been known to step on the red carpet from an Inter. class when the train was particularly full. The compartment to hold six was quite full when we started and overflowing before we left, as all Indians love trains and stations and the entire family always comes down to see the one travelling member off and sits in the compartment until the train starts to move — then there is the devil of a scramble and babies are handed thro' the windows and granny is hauled from the high steps!

Anyway, we were the only Europeans and our companions were *weird*. One little man was wearing a Ghandi hat on his black curly flowing locks, his hair was shoulder length, a gay waistcoat under a Norfolk jacket and voluminous dhoti which left lots of bare leg and sandals. Then there were a very beautiful young girl in a white sari with a rose in her hair, a small boy dressed up to the eyes in a khaki officer's suit, plus Brigadier's pips — he was just three we were told! — then the husband and father, a rather bloated and tipsy man in European suit and a grey-beard friend who promptly took to the top berth and went to sleep with his head on a rose-decorated tin trunk! The family and Ghandi-hat man were covered in garlands soaked in rose-water and the small boy spent his time sniffing all the flowers and putting them in his mother's hair. We smiled pleasantly and said 'how-do-you-do' to the silence after the train had started — Indians never like to start talking to Europeans, they are shy — and then we got well away and had the most enjoyable three hours possible.

The lovely girl was a film actress and the tipsy sot the Producer and the funny man was *really* the funny man on the films and also the most celebrated singer, Mr. Vishnu Sheoram Jog! After the Producer had offered everyone a tot from his whisky-bottle and we had offered everyone English cigarettes I suggested that Mr. Jog sang for us as I don't really understand Indian music. He obliged at once and sang charmingly. In three hours we had to change into the bigger train to our coupé for the night and really I was most sorry to say goodbye. They invited us to come to the film studio in Bombay where they would be shooting a new film in two days time, but unfortunately we hadn't time and our four days were full to overflowing, once we reached Bombay.

Calcutta, 1947

Poor England does seem to be having the most extraordinary weather possible — we read in today's paper that the Easter holiday weather has been very cold and rainy. It is frightful after all the snow and ice and then floods. We, here in Calcutta, are having unprecedented heat for April and yesterday the temperature in the

Hasting's House, Calcutta.

shade was 104° and likely to get hotter until we have a 'North-Easter' which usually means that one has to put up the wooden slatted shutters before ten o'clock, then over them the long French windows to try and keep the heat out. Of course this puts all the rooms in total darkness and so we stay, the electric fans whizzing and everything

Sir William Jones's tomb.

Unfinished study of bronze gates.

Rose Aylmer's tomb.

tightly shut, until about seven o'clock in the evening, when the sun goes down. The streets are like furnaces and the heat from the outside balconies is soaked up in the masonry all day, so that there is a hot blast as soon as the shutters are open. We ourselves just drip and *drip* — already I have had *two* complete changes of clothes since breakfast and shall probably have to have another before tea.

Did I tell you that we have a small white kitten, which we rescued from a horrid death? We call her Daisy and she is growing fast and seems to love us as much as we do her. She comes to Geoffrey's whistle like a dog and bounds along! At present she is sitting on a table in rapt admiration of two small green parrots we have. They are quite safe from her as their cage is a very big wicker one, like a dome, and all the cool hours they are on the veranda, but after lunch I bring them in. They sit on their perch, twittering to each other and holding their lovely red beaks together, most lovingly.

I have been reading in 'Vogue' and other English

Old chandelier.

Council chamber.

*Throne Room,
Government House.*

magazines lately that to wear a cameo brooch and ear-rings is the smartest thing possible and I am hoping that when we are home you may be able to find me a spare cameo among your old ornaments. They are so beautiful and look just right pinned on a lapel. Owing to this torrid heat I just cannot bear my hair on my neck any longer and so have put it up. It is only just long enough not to have trailing ends and no doubt will improve when it grows more — the ends are on the top of my head in curls, and really I am cool and look rather chic, everyone says. Here in India, unless I am going to church or a wedding or the races, I never wear a hat — nor does anyone else — just have a sunshade and sun glasses, so what I shall do about a hat when at home I don't know. The kind of hat that looked right on long bobbed hair will not look good on 'Up' hair, will it?

Warren Hasting's throne.

*Calcutta,
May 1947*

Yellow drawing-room, Government House.

Sunday morning and the start of another day of intense heat and *drip.* To you at home, who have never been more than 'comfortably'

Tipu Sultan's throne.

hot, this Calcutta temperature of 107-8-9- with a humidity of about 100 per cent is impossible to magine, but I can assure you it is utter misery. Day after day, one drips while one dresses and before I have had time to put on a dress my one undergarment is sopping around the waist and before I have had my dress on for ten minutes, the front and back are dark with drip, my face pours in rivulets down to my neck and I have to have relays of face tissues with which to mop the whole time. I am describing ME — but it applies to everyone one sees or meets — this year Geoffrey and I are lucky not to have Prickly Heat, which is an irritating red rash that comes everywhere and is caused by salty sweat blocking the pores. I have a shower in tepid water every hour or so and G. has a change and shower at lunch-time and before he returns to the office and again at 4.45 when he comes back and at intervals till bed-time, and, of course, every shower means a change of clothes.

      The proper uniform for British troops in Calcutta is just shorts and stockings and boots. When we go into the Fort it is quite lovely to see all these healthy-looking browned bodies, the higher ranks wearing an armband on their bare arms, which is a bit comic, and to see them on point-duty is most amusing. It seems a little odd to have the Military Police half-naked but it does stop Prickly Heat, which is the object of the order. Just how those marvellous old soldiers, dressed in tight red high-buttoned stuff clothes *marched* across the plains of India and fought battles at the end of a day's march — June in the Punjab during the Siege of Delhi, for instance — is beyond belief.

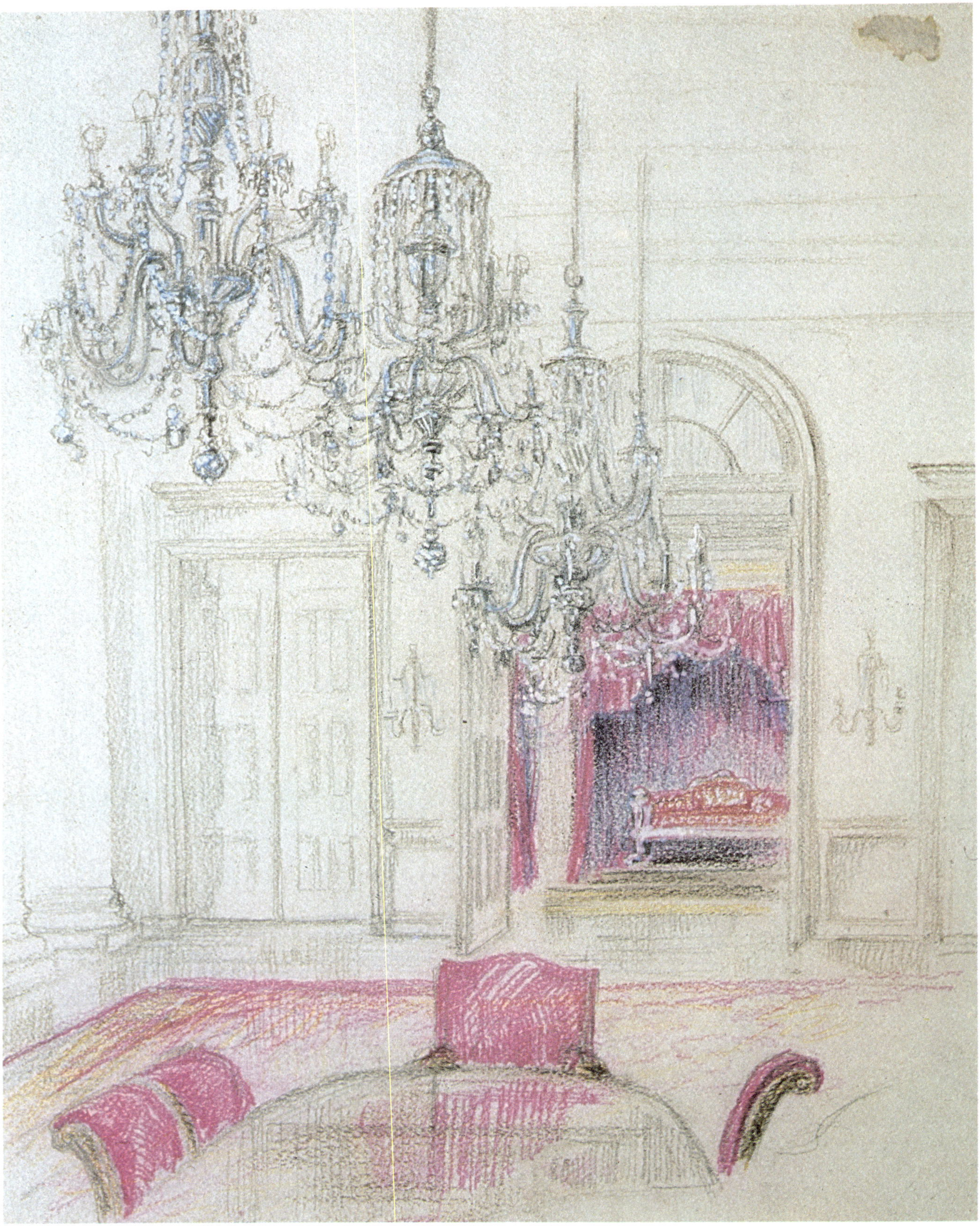

Government House, Calcutta

I have thought of you a lot lately, you who know how to draw interiors and can do a good perspective, while I have been most laboriously making sketches of Government House. Although the newspapers say 'Not since Cecil Beaton came to take photographs years ago have these historic interiors been so artistically portrayed' etc., really it is a case of Doctor Johnson's Dog and an opportunity wasted on me, if there had been someone better, as interiors are *not* my line of country.

As you may remember, India before 1911 was always governed from Calcutta, and this huge and lovely Govt. House was built at the very beginning of the nineteenth century modelled on Keddleston and is very imposing, as it is intended to be. The main rooms are huge and very well proportioned, the drawing-rooms and Throne Room having great cream-coloured columns at each end and the dining-room, which makes the long stroke of a T, and the Throne Room, which has them down each side, are most imposing. On Durbar days the procession starts there and works forward to the distance where the old 'Warren Hastings Throne' stands on a dais under a canopy of white and gold with red hangings. The throne itself is fascinating; of silver, upholstered in pink and gold Indian brocade and has arms of large silver lions — almost life-size — their eyes of topaz and between them is space for quite three Governors. Warren Hastings is said to have filched it from some native ruler. In the same room is a quite tiny throne of gold leaf, with a small footstool, which belonged to wicked Tipu Sultan, the 'Tiger' of Mysore. All the rooms are hung with rows of the most lovely old crystal chandeliers I have ever seen and the effect of so many is fairy-like and ethereal — but they are devilish to put onto paper. The old Council Chamber is brown and leather and has great wide padded chairs, comfortable for all-night sittings and I sat myself firmly in the Governor's seat, thinking that Warren Hastings had himself sat there so long ago.

Last year when I was in Kalimpong I made quite a lot of coloured-pencil sketches of the rickety houses and bazaar streets and now I find, thro' an advertising man who has seen the sketches, that the Railway Co. would like one or two for posters. There is one particular one, for which I had to climb a roof and look down to the roofs, that they have asked me to do and so I am busy, clad in a bather, working under a fan with dripping face and body, turning the small sketch into full poster size — not so easy without easel and proper room to move in but it is coming on. The poor blind kitten that we chanced upon the other day and brought to our room lies around my feet and as it can't see me I have to be careful not to tread on it — it is *most* pathetic; one eye just a socket, no eyeball and the other sightless. It was starving of course and Geoffrey will have to destroy it, I am afraid, but it is now comparatively happy with us for a few weeks.

Facing page: Throne room, Government House.

Calcutta

We now live in the Grand Hotel and have a three-roomed suite. The nice sitting-room has a veranda which looks over the Maidan and on to the river Hooghly and all the shipping. We are three floors up and so get the cool breezes and miss all the heat and a lot of the noise from Chowringhee, the main thoroughfare of Calcutta which borders the Maidan. The latter is a vast green plain, dotted with big banyan and pepal-trees, some small 'tanks' or lakes and intersected with roads for the traffic. The Indians all graze their cattle on the grass and the old black buffaloes wallow in the muddy bits for hours and then quite suddenly emerge from their sludgy patch, dripping mud and rivulets of dirty water. Unlike ordinary cows, they have TWO ROWS of great white most false-looking teeth and they have a habit of slightly opening their mouths and grinning at one — quite terrifying to see half a ton of hideous black flesh suddenly look animated!

Up to now we have always lived in the more residential areas of Calcutta among the big two-storeyed white bungalows, many of them built by the old 'John Company' and beautifully proportioned, but now we are on the main boulevard and in the biggest hotel and quite a different life surrounds us. In the dining-room we have our own reserved table in a corner where we can see all that comes and goes without being in it ourselves. Everyday there are new faces as the travellers come off the planes and the ships. Some people have tired and hot little children — the table Khitmutgars love these infants and cluster like crows around them, the (usually) yellow-headed children just lapping up all the attention — it makes me laugh.

On the pavement outside the entrance there is a long arcade over to the road and so, being three-up, all noise from there is considerably deadened and we see nothing but the road — *but,* to be down there at any time of the day or night is an education in itself. A continuous loud hum of vendors is at top-pitch all the time and the men who sell puppy-dogs, parakeets and love-birds; the boys who polish shoes; the masses of creatures selling magazines and papers; the flower-sellers; the pan-sellers and peanut-vendors and last but certainly not least the boys who have Indian flutes — whistle things — to sell and, as bait, play them eternally (usually the same tune of 'Bicycle made for two') so that this thin squeak sometimes even penetrates into the road and the traffic and I hear it on the stiller nights.

When the ships from home are in and all the sailors with their white duck trousers and navy hats saying H.M.S. are around there is even more of a haroosh and they get into drunken arguments with the rickshaw men and a real set-to starts. I forgot to tell you, the only noise I really like is the incessant clonk-clonk of the rickshaw men — as they run they beat a little brass bell, minus its clapper, onto the shafts of the rickshaw; it goes on eternally and they must do it in

The Raja of Puri.

The maidan, Calcutta.

their sleep I should think and it is really rather pleasant. Now, as I write, I can hear the noise of a small kettle-drum which means that the 'Monkeyman' and his two poor little creatures are probably entertaining the crowd — that whir of drums is their recognised sound, the same as the balloon man has *his* recognised noise. I find it all fascinating, tho' I haven't a doubt that it would drive most people crackers.

The Raja's son.

Puri

June 24th, 1947

Our holiday at Puri, which is on the coast, was most interesting and we were lucky enough to be there at the time of the Jagganath Car festival. We thought that it was in May, but found it was last week. You have probably heard of it, but did you know that there were *three* cars? I didn't. Puri is the home of the huge and ancient Jagganath temple and in it 'live' the three gods, Jagganath, his elder brother Balaram and their sister Sabatra. The Hindus regard them as all being exceedingly holy, but Jagganath most of all and thousands

83

of pilgrims journey from the far ends of the country for this festival. Every year the three great wooden blocks, with primitive faces, rather like the Easter Island gods on the steps of the British Museum but painted bright colours, are taken from their temple and put onto three specially constructed wooden cars, vast things taller than any house, with sixteen wheels a-piece. These gods are so heavy that it takes eight coolies of prize-fighting physique to bring each one in stages from the temple to the cars. They are then towed by the populace, who all haul on the thick hawsers until the tower-decorated edifice gets under way, down the broad village street to another temple about a mile and a half away. There they stay for nine days and then the process is repeated in the reverse direction.

The ambition of each pilgrim is to touch the gods. To do this they mill around in endless masses, waiting to be allowed up the broad wooden ramps leading to each car. They fight, they yell, the police try and keep order and the stretcher bearers come to pick up the injured and to save them from being trampled underfoot. The crowd was said to number a *hundred thousand* and it certainly looked like it — a positive sea of black faces, mainly white clothes with a touch of pink and orange and green and blue for shirts here and there, a purple sari perhaps and the bright red pugarees of the Police.

A corner of Puri.

The three Jagganath cars.

I have always heard that if a pilgrim can get himself crushed under the wheels of Jagganath, he will go straight to his final Heaven. It seemed a far-fetched idea that anyone would be so mad as to do this — but during the time the cars were being towed, four people were killed, wilfully or not. Masses crowd onto the structure of these primitive cars, sitting and clinging to the under-beams, and of course they may get jolted off as there is no method of steering with just ropes pulling. An old man was the first, and a young policeman nearly lost his life in trying to save him — both were put on stretchers below us, the old man quite dead; horrible.

Elephant gateway.

Temple in Puri.

The Monkey Temple.

The Monkey Shrine.

85

The Raja of Puri, whose forebears built the gigantic temple in the ninth century, was extremely kind and gave us his own special seats on a roof-top so that I should have the best possible view for sketching and Geoffrey for his camera — so we have a lot of records of this truly unique festival. We sat in those basket-chairs from just after 9 a.m. until 6 p.m. without moving — the hotel had packed us sandwiches for lunch and we had a Thermos of water. Anyway, if we had wanted to go back to the hotel we couldn't have done so — it was utterly impossible for anyone to move in the crowd. It was most interesting and I wouldn't have missed it for anything, as it is a ceremony that remains unaltered since the temple was founded.

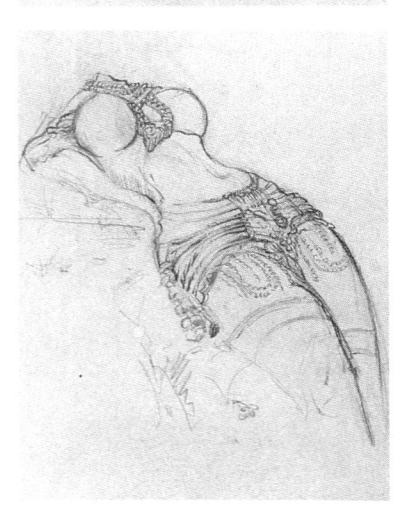

Konorak

All illustrations: Fallen statuary at Konorak.

An adventure came again when we did a trip by bullock-cart over the desert for thirty miles to see the even older 'Black Pagoda' at Konorak. It is mainly in ruins but that which is left has been covered by the shifting sands for centuries and now, since 1890, the Archaeological Society has been doing a marvellous job of digging out and preservation, so that one can see what a wonder it has been. Experts say it is more interesting than Angkor Wat, so we went to look. It is a very difficult journey, as there is no motor road and the traditional way is by bullock-cart, the idea being that one gets into the hooded cart in the evening and sleeps till early morning, when Konorak is reached; but like so many things in this country, it just didn't work out like that and we spent many hours getting there and had a most exhausting time, almost giving up — but not quite! As there is no road what-so-ever, the bullock man lost his way, and amongst other things we had to walk behind the cart in a red-hot wind and blinding sandstorm for miles — had to ford a waist-deep river on foot as the bullocks were not strong enough and generally push and heave the cart along. Every bit of food and water had to be taken with us, as there is only a tiny Dak bungalow there — no village — and I cooked our meals myself. We started about six o'clock in the evening and walked, with very small intervals of taking it in turns to rest in the jolting bullock-cart until about 3 a.m. when, utterly lost and the lamp of the cart out, we called a halt till dawn. At 5 a.m. we went off again, trying to get to the ford at least before the heat but the sand-storm and the wind which really *hurt* and the sun all beat us. Even when we could see the far distant top of the temple in a thicket of trees, it took us four hours before we were there, so slow were the bullocks and so deceptive the distance. Why it is named the Black Pagoda I don't know, as the great blocks of hewn stone that make it are honey coloured. Some Sadhus have a little old temple near the biggest banyan-tree I have ever seen and in the dusk they ring their clanging bells and clatter their tiny cymbals, to add to the few noises in the quiet.

The temple is carved from the ground level upwards, mostly with figures of dancing-girls and gods, sometimes with friezes of war elephants and horses, but all of it virile, exciting and perfect in technique. The roof is roughly pyramid in shape, going up in steps and tiers and has a row of larger-than-life figures of dancing-girls half way up. The grace of these is delightful. Some have fallen onto the grass a hundred or so feet below and tho' they have lost their heads and an arm or leg the beauty of the modelling is a joy — truly it must have been a golden age in India, as nothing like it has been done since. There are two vast horses at one entrance and it was only when I was sketching them (in the early sun of 5 a.m. next morning) that I could fully appreciate the marvel of their art — not the detailed classic of the Greeks or Romans, but more of what Epstein must be trying for, in their boldness of outline, and yet every muscle, every wave of their manes and every detailed curve that their harness and trappings covered was a perfect bit of sculpting. They are about eighth century.

We could have stayed there for weeks, and we did stay an extra night but our food and water were running short and there was no way of getting more. The jolly fat Raja had originally offered us his State elephants as 'mounts' but these I had refused as riding in a howdah is so joggly and sixty odd miles would have been too much for me. Coming back we caught up with another cart which was taken the Archaeological Representative to civilisation and he had two huge white bullocks with collars of ringing jingling bells, quite lovely to hear thro' the darkness — with them was a Sadhu, a great tall man who strode ahead like a warrior, his beard and long hair streaming in the wind and his red dhoti wrapping around his long legs. He talked a little to us and seemed most unusually charming and 'Good' — a contrast to the usual filthy Sadhu with ash-whitened face and the red eyes of the opium eater. The next day when we told the Raja about him, he said he was the brother of a Rajput prince who had given up everything to become a priest — he certainly looked it.

The Raja insisted upon us coming to lunch with him on the morning I sketched him and his son for a memento portrait and we ate our mountain of rice and curry off huge silver trays with small silver bowls of different foods set around it. He and his sons ate with their fingers after he, for politeness, had started with a spoon and fork for our benefit and a servant stood at each end of the table with an enormous Arabian Nights' fan of Peacock's feathers to wave over us. Afterwards I was taken thro' antique and tortuous stone passages to the Purdah quarters, and I met and talked with the Rani — a really lovely woman, tho' a little fat. She was most beautifully dressed in an ice-cream pink Benares sari and little jewelled slippers. Tho' her sons and husband speak perfect English, she only understood a little and couldn't speak so we had to find some Hindustani for conversation — but I did like her.

Karachi, 1947

You have probably read of the wonderful time we have been having here, and of the historic ceremonies of 'Handing over' by Lord Mountbatten and the Flag Hoisting ceremony by Mr. Jinnah, who must have been profoundly stirred to see the green flag of Pakistan, with its star and crescent, fluttering above the parade ground and on the top of Government House — a wonderful day for him. He is very charming, a quite old man unfortunately, but so dignified and with such a wonderful grip on everything. One of the nice things he did was to fly the Union Jack as well as his own flag on Independence Day and all the Europeans and Indians got along most happily together, no ill-feeling — we are a marvellous race, we *really* are.

At the wonderful reception at Government House for the Mountbattens, we all wore long gloves and looked as 'courtly' as possible. The gardens were lit up with fairy-lights in the trees and there was a wonderful display of firework rockets that looked like diamond necklaces coming down from the dark skies. Bands played on the lawns where they walked after the reception and everywhere were the tall Indian Lancers of the Bodyguard, motionless with their lances straight beside them. The saris and satin trousers and tunics and gauzy veils that the Indian ladies wore were fairy-like and, of course, all the European women had their best dresses and long gloves. I wore a blue dress which has a black bead decoration across the draped bodice — looks a bit like great black feathers — and long black gloves and handbag. I am the fortunate possessor of more than one pair of long gloves and I can assure you all my spares were leant out in no time to my friends as none of the little shops here stock them, and now I wear my hair piled on top, which is more dignified. Geoffrey was in uniform, but he was one of the few, as most men are now in civilian dress and wear the tropical evening dress of white jacket and black trousers.

The row of cars was worthy of the Mall and Buckingham Palace Courts — everyone in a twitter to be early and no one achieving it on account of the crowds. The big lawns and trees at G.H. were lovely that night — small lights in all the trees and flood-lighting on the house and the terrace and steps. At odd intervals were the Vice-regal Bodyguard men immobile, their lances at their sides, while red-and-gold-coated Sindi servants did their best to keep up the province's morale. The Baluchi Band with its cherry-red trousers and white spats, plaid over shoulder and gorgeous turbans played at the foot of the steps and the Europeans and Indians all stood about on the lawn, waiting for the Mountbattens and the Jinnahs to show themselves.

The Indian women's saris were simply superb — fairy gossamer things from Benares, fragile as cobwebs and showing their little satin blouses and glinting jewellery. Sind, being Muslim, has a particularly pretty dress for the women, very full gathered trousers, a long tunic and over the head and shoulders a gauzy veil. The younger women have started a new fashion and, instead of the great satin 'shalwars' that their mothers were wearing, they had very wide divided skirts of taffeta, which have an even wider frill from the knees down, mainly embroidered with sequins or silver and gold thread. Their ear-rings hang down to their shoulders and they all wear excellent make-up, but with the added charm of kohl-rimmed eyes — it suits them but would make us look terrible!

The men were wearing the Muslim achkan, a long tight-buttoned waisted coat to the knees and either ordinary white trousers or the baggy shalwar. There were Khan Sahibs from Upper Sind there too, and they were in enormous white shalwars, tent-like coats and had about twenty yards of white turban on their black and bushy heads, but were most picturesque and fierce to look at.

At last we mounted the steps for our presentations, Lord and Lady Mountbatten, the Quaid-i-Azam and Miss Fatima Jinnah (sister) standing in that order, surrounded by cinema photographers and studio lights, A.D.C.s and Bodyguard.

As our turn came and the A.D.C. roared forth our names, Lord M. gave a most charming smile and handshake for my curtsy, then the same from 'Edwina' and then handshakes from the Jinnahs and it was over and we could go and drink iced coffee in the cool again. I had never seen Lord M. before — he looked extremely handsome in white naval uniform — but I had met Lady M. in 1944 when she gave me tea and asked me to go to Bangalore and paint murals. She was wearing a pale green lamé dress and carried a huge emerald-green ostrich feather fan. Around her neck was a blazing row of enormous diamonds and emeralds, which looked as tho' they were on fire as they glinted in the white arc lights, and her bracelets were the same — I have never seen such wonderful jewels. The four of them stood there for over an hour, receiving and smiling and

Awaiting events on 'Handover' Day.

shaking hands, on one of the hottest nights. It must have worn them out by the end of it — afterwards they all walked in the gardens chatting to people. We met our old friend the Rao Rajah Hanut Singh, the great polo-player. Hanut and Lord M. are old friends and he had just been talking to him and had said 'Hanut, fighting the war was *nothing* to the job I have now! — one can well believe it.

As the band played all the English and Scotch melodies they had ever known the fireworks started, and against the dark blue night-sky the spark-trailing rockets looked like more of Lady Mountbatten's diamonds dropping against the stars, quite *quite* lovely — it was a marvellous evening!

The next morning, early in the warm sunshine, troops and naval boys, both Indian and European, were all lined up outside the Assembly Buildings to meet the Mountbattens and the Jinnahs for the historic 'Handing-over' ceremony. This was done inside the big hall, and we had the choice of being inside and only seeing a bit or staying outside and seeing all the rest; so we did the latter and I made as many sketches as I could in the time, propped up against a shady tree by the band of the Royal Scots. Lord M. was again in Naval uniform and she in a long white dress with a tiny hat of white flowers and they both wore blue orders over their shoulders. The green flag of Pakistan, crescent and star in white, flew up over the buildings and everywhere there were triumphal arches, each named after some famous Muslim and everywhere decorated with bunting and rows of small green flags of paper. Some of the crowd, all very good-tempered and cheering occasionally at everything or nothing, climbed into a nearby tree which partly collapsed with the sheer weight of numbers and they were flung to the ground as the Mountbattens stepped with Mr. Jinnah onto the red carpet — great fun!

This day being the historic Fifteenth, there was the Flag Hoisting ceremony in the afternoon, when the Quaid-i-Azam (Jinnah's title now) reviewed the Army and Navy on the parade ground, after which the flag of Pakistan was hoisted. It must have been the most *wonderful* moment for Mr. Jinnah who is now rather old and frail — seventy-three to be exact. He has won all hearts by his intense sincerity and uprightness of character, his good sense and manners, so different from those of Hindustan in every way. For the whole day of the 15th (*his* day) he had our Union Jack flying alongside the flag of Pakistan — a grand gesture. So was his idea of coming to Holy Trinity Church, with his sister and the Muslim Governor and Staff on the following Sunday, when the Archbishop of Sind held a Dominion Sunday Service, with special sets of prayer and lessons. It must have been practically the first time that a devout Mohammedan has gone to a service in a Christian church. It was tremendously appreciated and the church was full to overflowing and our naughty little choirboys were all wearing red cassocks and had clean frills and lace on their white shirts!

The Governor, Geoffrey's old friend fat Sheik Gulam Hussein, has given dinners and parties, (he waved the A.D.C. who was about to announce G. with 'No introduction — Swayne-Thomas is

Jinnah and the Mountbattens on 'Handover' Day.

an old friend of mine' — so nice!). Miss Jinnah has had Purdah Parties, at which I have sat in baking sun trying to look as tho' I was enjoying the 'Pink tea' and inane chatter. It was pleasant tho' when all the young Muslim maidens stood dressed in white baggy shalwars, long white tunics, their hair in braids down their backs and the green scarf of the Muslim League tied from shoulder to waist. They formed a double-rowed guard of honour for Fatima Jinnah and as she passed tore the petals from the flowers they held in their hands and scattered them at her feet. Some of the matriarchal Muslim dames are *vast,* and when wrapped in satins and scarves look like whales dressed up. Purdah women of the old school get no exercise what-so-ever and even when young and 25-ish, run to wobbly fat, but not all, I saw one or two exquisitely lovely young things that afternoon, beautifully dressed.

Two nights later the Jinnahs gave an almost identical reception at Govt. House, where, after the 'Handover' on the 15th, they now live. Odd to see the Muslim flag instead of the Union Jack — and Miss Jinnah, the sister, gave a huge garden party about three days ago.

As you may have seen in the paper, great rioting and killing and looting and arson have broken out in the Punjab and now in Quetta — trains from Bengal and Delhi have been derailed and the occupants, still alive, have been brutally butchered. It is all ghastly — I dread taking up a newspaper — but here, in Sind, it is all calm and quiet and everybody is friendly and happy; no demonstrations and the outgoing British and the in-coming Indians are all *most* friendly and happy together, and this is very fine and good. Long may it last. As a precautionary measure there was a display of force by the entire Baluch Regt. in full fighting kit, around the town this morning — but in most other parts the news is simply dreadful and mostly on account of the Partition, which is vastly unpopular. The refugees from the East Punjab now number over a quarter of a million, the death roll is in the four figure category, and there are wholesale massacres around Lahore. Trains are daily overturned, and so now a great many train services have been suspended completely. One or two have been burnt to cinders, the refugee passengers first being brutally murdered, and the one train containing the Pakistan Government's baggage burnt up, too. Delhi is choc-a-bloc with refugees and the food problem must be more than acute. Jinnah leaves for Lahore this morning to try and do something, but all the newspapers agree that the 'Other side' — Hindustan — 'is not pulling their whole weight' to quote from a headline.

There are very few Hindus here, and everything seems so peaceful and under control that one hopes there will not be retaliations — but yesterday, as Geoffrey was coming into the gates in his car, a Hindu came running after him and begged for his help. He and his family live in a Muslim quarter (where isn't it, here?) and four days ago while this man was out a number of men came and beat up his wife and children and carried off his little daughter, who has now been returned more dead than alive.

We were told by the B.O.A.C. people who flew Sir Fred Burrows off for Calcutta on the 15th morning I think, after the 'Handover' there, that the poor man had a terrible time — an enormous crowd broke into Government House grounds, the Police being unwilling or incapable of stopping them, and that they got hold of poor Fred and put Ghandi hats on his defenceless head, made him wave a Congress flag and thoroughly mobbed him. They swarmed all over the beautiful Government House and did damage to the sum of thousands of rupees to all those lovely and irreplaceable treasures that abound — thank Heaven I sketched what I did, in May — and generally mobbed the place. Fred escaped, feeling thankful that he wasn't more than bruised and shaken.

In Delhi on the 15th, the crowd also got out of hand and the brother of a great friend of ours here, a Brig. in the 10th Gurkhas, said he lost sight of his tiny men altogether and eventually they had to be re-paraded. They didn't like the idea of the 'Handover' anyway, and had nearly mutinied and wouldn't parade for a while — odd. But the crowd in Delhi was good-tempered, tho' when it saw a very tall officer standing near to our Brig. they decided he was the Auk and mobbed him, sticking little pin-flags with Congress colours

The princes' residences.

all over the poor man, *and* into him, so that he was like a sore pincushion!

You no doubt see the tales of frightfulness in your own papers and read of the lines, fifty miles long, of helpless refugees who trek from one province to another, their poor little possessions on their backs and the whole column sometimes wiped out by the opposite religion who come armed with swords and knives. This has happened on refugee trains too; 3,000 men, women and children unarmed and helpless were butchered in less than two hours outside Amritsar a fortnight ago by armed Sikhs who descended onto the held-up train and, with fearful method, killed practically everyone and the few who lived to tell the tale were buried beneath corpses and taken for dead. Before that, all Sikhs had left Pakistan, all of them, both wealthy and poor, so that there should be no retaliation. We all, on hearing of the exodus, felt that something untoward was brewing — later we knew and now all Hindus are going. Every day they leave in their hundreds, in ships from the port, to travel to Bombay by sea and half the shops are shuttered and deserted; the dirzees, sweepers — sorry — tailors, cleaners, gardeners and the like, who are usually of the Hindu religion, have all gone or are going even tho' they are assured of safety and protection.

Benares

I must tell you about our trip to Benares, which was about three weeks ago, before the journey became too unbearably hot — but Benares has a crackling dry heat with the usual afternoon sandstorm, it was so then. It is an overnight journey, arriving about 11 a.m. next day. There had been a great deal of trouble in the city and in the cantonment and lots of stabbing deaths. There was just one European hotel in the almost deserted cantonment and we were the only guests — in fact we saw just one other European in the whole place while were there and he was a Swiss traveller; one gets quite used to seeing only Indians everywhere.

We hired the hotel car and a Guide and set forth to see all that was holy and of interest. Khasi is the Indian name for the place and at festival times the whole of this side of India and every pious Hindu who can afford it come to bathe themselves in the Sacred Ganges. As you probably know, the Buddha did a great deal of his preaching around Benares, and we went first to the temple set in the Deer Park where he started his teachings. The ancient Buddhists built a huge Stupa there and, of course, being solid it is still standing, and as vast as ever. Nearby is the 'dig' of ancient monasteries and a nunnery; and all that has been unearthed from it is

A tonga.

stored in a nice new museum close by — wonderful carved figures of men and animals, quite lovely.

The walls of the temple were covered with twice-life-sized murals shewing scenes from the Holy Life — they were done by a Japanese artist in 1932-6 and they are simply superb — he seems to have really studied the human figure from a model instead of just inventing a cardboard shape, as an Indian would have done. I was very impressed. At one end was the altar with a vast golden Buddha sitting cross-legged, as I saw often in the temples of Sikkim last year, and have sketched. The many incidents in the murals were taken direct in costume and pose from the lovely stone statues and friezes that had recently been dug up. We then left Sarnath, which is the name of the place, and went to look at a new Hindu temple called 'Mother India' — but as I had to take off my shoes and walk barefoot for quite a long way before getting into the place (old Gandhi opened it in 1926) I refused. I don't in the least mind going barefoot *inside* a Buddhist or Muslim temple, but I will be hanged if I will go to unnecessary lengths for Hindus, who have such utterly filthy ways in temples and everything they do — NO! So for the first time, I missed something.

The native town itself is dirty and bedraggled and poor-looking and the two most important shops, which have sent their lovely saris and woven fabrics to the Exhibition in London, are tiny, and found in the corner of a winding little street. But, the saris — it seemed almost impossible that any human hands could have gone to their making, some were so fragile that only the golden threads stood out when they were tossed up and fell into billows of gossamer against the light. Afterwards, we went to the tiny hovels where men and little boys sit in small pits, weaving during the daylight hours in the greatest of discomfort imaginable. The workings of the hand-looms are most intricate and I'll swear the weavers, who start when they are six or seven years old, work mainly from instinct — tho' we were shown some small nitzy-bitzy papers which they said were the original designs. I spent my time with a sketch-book in hand, and one of my sitters was the father of the proprietor, an old blind weaver of eighty-nine. He sat with his back to a wall, softly mumbling, surrounded by masses of the most brightly coloured silks that he couldn't see, and asked his son to request that we would shake hands with him before we went.

The next morning we were up very early, and before the furnace-like heat had started were down in a car to the sacred Ganges — there was a small trouble just as we were starting, as the Guide had forgotten to tell the driver, who was a Muslim, where we were going, and he discovered that it was to be a Hindu quarter of the City. So, we had to wait until a fresh driver, Hindu caste, was found. There had been great trouble and stabbing and so the Guide, who was a Muslim too, had dressed himself up in khaki and was wearing a topee as the Anglo-Indians do. He spent most of his time asking what we thought would happen to him in 1948, and was certain, poor man, that he would be killed as soon as the British had

The blind weaver.

departed — so are a great many of them.

The river is broad, brown and dirty and curves past the ghats and towers and palaces that fringe the streets of the city. The opposite banks are barren mud and small cargo boats with single square sail idle along on the stream. Awaiting us was a houseboat manned by two very old oarsmen and on the roof were three chairs for us and the Guide, who sat behind and breathed down our necks. It all seemed very top heavy and I felt that I dare not change seats or the whole boat would capsize and we should be in dirty Mother Ganges. The steep slopes of the banks are cobbled and have steps, lined with whining beggars. I opened and shut my sunshade at them all and they stopped whining and made off — long ago I found that in this country a sunshade has more uses than it was ever designed for! All over the bathing-ghats are propped large sunshades of palm matting, with a small sitting-place like a low table, beneath. Here the pious and faithful sit and contemplate or, if they are Sadhus and wrapped in tangerine-coloured garments, the pilgrims come to them for blessings and prayers. Some of the little platforms are built out into the stream, handy for bathing.

The little houseboat started and from mid-stream the early morning haze made everything look rather like Turner's painting of the Grand Canal. We first went upstream, passing enormous palaces hung with gaily painted balconies, vast tiers of steps leading to the river and bathing towers and galleries along the banks. Some of the steps were being used for drying pink, red, yellow and white sari lengths which had been washed and in the green-brown water lapping the steps were floating garlands of glowing marigolds. Boys, men and old gentlemen with shining brass lotas in their hands came bobbing and puffing up and then vanished again for another immersion while women stood waist deep, their saris and long black hair clinging to their wet bodies as they took their baths. Then we came to a rather derelict part of the banks, where the houses and towers were ruined. In the mud at the water's edge were countless slabs of beating stones and hundreds of dhobis were pounding and banging the whole of Benares city's washing, their donkeys standing patiently up the slopes waiting to take the return load of washing. We had never seen such a positive 'herd' of dhobis and Geoffrey did his best to take a snapshot of them in the pale morning mist, but I doubt if it has come out. Then our boatmen turned and we had a beautiful view of the curving river, the ghats covered with sunshades and the gaily painted small houseboats and gondola-like rowing boats that were lazily moving about. In the far distance stood the main landmark of the city — the fragile spires of the one Muslim mosque, which was originally a Hindu temple until the Emperor Arungzebe converted it and built a dome and minarettes.

As we neared the Burning Ghats we passed the truly unpleasant sight of a floating corpse and farther on the bodies of animals bobbing along beside us, the crows and kites making their breakfast off all of them. Then we reached the Burning Ghats, where

Weaving scenes.

huge heaps of wood were stacked and the Domes, the lower order of Untouchables who deal with corpses, were busy with their work amidst the blue smoke of the wood pyres. As plague, smallpox and cholera were all raging in the city (knowing this we had been well vaccinated and inoculated before we left Calcutta), there were many corpses about tied with rope to the bamboo poles that form a stretcher for the body — the women were covered with red and purple cloths and the men were white and these stretchers stood half-upright and partly submerged in the sacred Ganges, waiting their turn for burning. Stray cows and calves stood around quite un-noticed and we watched one go up to a corpse and start eating the straw rope that bound it to the bamboo poles, while another did unmentionable things into the water near by, rapidly making Mother Ganges more holy than ever, no doubt. Into the same water that the cows, corpses and what-not stood in, were pilgrims washing themselves, utterly submerging themselves and then drinking deep — but, as we always say, if there were not this urge on the part of India's teeming millions to drink and bathe in the obviously germ-laden waters, there would be even more of a food problem. As it is, Nature levels up, or would, if it were not for the interfering British who *will* try to cure the tubercula, vaccinate and inoculate and generally fight a wiser nature.

All the great Hindu Maharajas have their palaces along the banks, to which they come with all their wives and retainers during the sacred times of pilgrimage. The height of the walls of these buildings must be nearly a hundred feet or more as every monsoon the Ganges rises as much as thirty feet flooding all the lower storeys and leaving only the balconied tops clear of the water. What happens then to the bathers I don't know, as the steps of the ghats are, of course, entirely covered. There is a pontoon bridge higher up for wheeled traffic and camels and horses and the railway is carried by a simply colossal iron-girder bridge which is having a road added. It takes the train about five full minutes to cross and in that time I managed to make a sketch, looking down onto the tiny distant boats.

We also visited the famous Monkey Temple, sacred to the Goddess Durga who is Kali's sister — not quite such a horror as Kali, who is represented as a black figure, wearing a necklace of skulls, her hands blood-stained and her tongue out, eyes a goggle; but Durga is bad enough! There were literally hundreds and hundreds of monkeys of all sizes and an old and almost naked gentleman who was their guardian let me sketch him as he offered the thieving wretches nuts on a brass tray. We dared not put the camera, my sunshade or sketching things down for one second in case the King of the Monkeys came and thieved it.

Well, Calcutta has again a curfew and the civil war seems to have come too. The killings are not as bad as in August but the daily total that is published in the papers and for the past ten days says some hundreds have been killed and injured and the vultures sit on the

Guardian of the monkeys.

bare and dead tree on the Maidan opposite our window, waiting for the next corpse. I first saw them one early morning — not a pleasant start for a hot and turgid day — and they seem to have chosen that dead tree as their headquarters. The curfew is from 7.30 p.m. to 6 a.m. and the Dragoons and their tanks and armoured cars patrol the city all night. Three days ago I was sitting in a car waiting for a friend who had to collect her daily milk as it hadn't been delivered and a poor, inoffensive little Hindu who was sitting on the kerb across the road was stabbed — ripped in the tummy — by a passing Muslim and dis-embowelled. Horrible! The latter made off. In England the crowd would no doubt have tried to get him, but here the crowd ran for its life, leaving a deserted side-street and a dying man. The gharry-horses all moved off, and later the Army and the Police came up with an ambulance and the man was taken away. That Muslim, without doubt, had no personal spite against the Hindu — he had probably just vowed to kill a Hindu that morning and afterwards a Hindu would kill a Muslim in retaliation and so it goes on.

There have been no trains — the mode of conveyance for every office clerk among others — since *January*. The buses still run on the days when there isn't too much killing, and they are packed

Beside the Ganges.

Facing page:
Mural in the author's home.

Below left: Sari material drying by the Ganges.
Below right: The burning ghats.

inside and festooned outside with humanity. Added to this strike, which entails firms providing lorries for the transport of their employees and the office 'day' starting at 10 a.m. or later and finishing at 4 p.m. — there is a dock workers' strike which has also been going on since January, and will no doubt account for the non-arrival of your Christmas books and certainly does for the empty shops. Then the Sweepers say it isn't safe to clean the already filthy streets and overflowing garbage-tins and they strike. The School teachers, who only receive about a £1 a week and have to have expensively procured degrees are also on strike — in fact I can't really tell you who *isn't* on strike or how any business is carried on.

Our sitting-room is like a godown, being full to overflowing with crates, tin trunks and wooden boxes, now having the carpenter's final tap before they are sent down to the docks to go home. They should land at Liverpool and then will be sent on to London, and we hope and trust that nothing is going to be lost. I have made most detailed lists of each box's contents, in quadruplicate, and all our most treasured possessions will just have to take their chances. We are not allowed to take them with us when we do go home and, as a lot of trouble is expected shortly, the Army is speeding things up and sending out notices saying the belongings may be sent from Calcutta. If this hadn't happened, although from our windows we can see the funnels and masts of all the shipping about 200 yards away, all our belongings would have had to go right across India by train and then be sorted and probably lost and perhaps some of them stolen before they were put on a ship at Bombay. We ourselves must sail from Bombay, which is too stupid — but I don't know when that will be — our possessions will be home long before we arrive.

Part Two

1952 to 1954

Coolies, Karachi.

Karachi, 1952

It is the strangest thing in the world to return like this, and there is an oddness that I cannot quite explain, with memory coming back as patchily as a half-forgotten dream. When I hear again the high-pitched voices mingling with the slow jingle of bullock carts; the crazy blare of the tea-shop radios in the bazaars; when chiels whistle and grey-headed crows caw-caw against the sunny blueness; then I thrill with a secret excitement and each day is a fresh adventure of the senses.

This morning we were on deck at 3.30 a.m. so that no moment could be missed and, when the Pilot came abroad, the far away lights of the port were glittering like sequins against the grey dawn. Much later, breakfast and goodbyes; in the turmoil of boxes and suitcases and coolies, I found myself shaking hands with the quite unknown uniformed representative of a travel firm, who had come aboard to see to somebody's luggage!

Passing the Customs was like a social visit, as the Officials rushed upon G. to shake him by the hand. A handsome and bearded young Pakistani officer thought to make conversation with me:

'And how are all the kiddies now?'

'But we have no children, you know. That is our misfortune.'

'But the Colonel looks young and strong and his passport says he is only forty-five years.'

I, wildly put to shame: 'It is I who am the unfortunate, and for my husband to have a family, another wife is necessary.'

Being a Muslim, he understands this point of view and I am spared more embarrassing details in defence of the male virility! Here, in the East, children are the only reason for the married state and if one wife cannot produce them another must, up to the third and fourth. It is kind of these people to be pleased to see us again and this first welcome seems like a homecoming. But I must brush up my

Urdu so that I can hold real conversations. For the moment we are to live in a hotel, and when a bungalow is found in Hyderabad we shall make that our headquarters. Once, long ago, we spent a happy year in the Cantonment of that strange city, which used to be called the Paris of the East, because of its beautiful Amil girls, but now that these gaily dressed Hindus and their families have fled, it must be very changed.

The Prophet's Birthday

December 1st

Today is a most auspicious one — the Muslim Christmas Day as you might say and a public holiday. From the first sunlight this morning the Maidan has been thronged with youths as they play cricket, hockey, football and more cricket, while the chiels and crows have wheeled above, scared by the noise of Jet Fighters which zoom over the Governor-General's house and garden.

At the farther end of the Maidan near to the lovely bit of Hindu architecture that was once a wealthy Club, the Governor's Bodyguard has played polo. There are birthday lights everywhere, outlining all the big building in coloured bulbs and neon and 'Happy Birthday' in Hindustani script sprawls across the top of Government House in twelve-foot-high letters. Our hotel is also gay with coloured lights and a full moon is coming up.

In the streets, vendors of pink sugar cakes and sweetmeats push little carts on bicycle wheels, topped by a frilly canopy and lit with flares as harsh as their voices. Along under the trees, men with bright blue enamel tea-pots sell tea in small cups. The tea is so hot that the customers, squatting on their heels around the charcoal fire, are obliged to pour it into their saucers and blow upon it before they drink with deeply appreciative sucking noises. Six inches away, the cars and rickshaws whizz past, all glare and noise.

Change

Karachi

How this city has changed since Partition! In the old days of the war and, now I remember it, Petrol Rationing, our mode of transport was the Victoria, drawn by a not-very-fast-moving horse. But this leisurely clop-clop has nearly vanished and masses of huge and hideous American taxi-cars rush and shriek all day and more than half the night, the main idea being to spare the brakes and drive on the horn.

To all this truly frightful din add both pedal and motor rickshaw, gaudy as Amazon parrots and ten times as noisy, as the men ring bells and toot squeaky horns incessantly. So many blocks of flats and houses have been built since we left, and the long vistas of sand dune and desert country are now covered with concrete buildings looking for all the world like pink and blue and yellow iced cakes.

But in a changing world there is still the camel cart, bringing merchandise from the Port. It is a lowish lorry with pneumatic tyres, and is drawn by the tall Sindi 'oonts' (camels), their heads a-bob as the drivers race them down the crowded roads. There is a story of a young man in a mini car, who, being held up by a traffic jam of these carts, just drove under the nearest camel's tummy and went triumphantly on!

Refugees by their homeless thousands still throng the pavements, waste lands and even tree-trunks, building pathetic shelters of reed matting, sacking and battered petrol tins against walls or ditches. Here they live in grime and filth because of the lack of water, eking out a hand-to-mouth existence by making cane furniture, selling fruit and vegetables or just begging. After six years the Government is still at a loss to provide for these Pakistanis. Formerly, many of them were people of substance; and having had to flee from India and renounce all their possessions and lands they now battle for mere survival. In most cases the Hindu had his wealth in cash which could be banked in his own country; but the majority of Muslims were agriculturalists and as their land was wealth they had to depart as poor men; and up to now without compensation.

Geoffrey's work, under the Colombo Plan is to plan new towns to house them — and a new Capital City for Sind near Hyderabad. We go to live in Hyderabad in about two weeks' time when an office will be ready, staff selected and our bungalow ready. We have been up there for five days and just come back; we used to live there in 1940 and know the city well.

Boxing Day 1952 (from Geoffrey)

This morning went out with the Ridleys to the desert where we were the guests of a big Zemindar family, the Nawab Jam Jan Mohammed Khan and his sons — eldest son, Nawabsadah Jam Amirali Khan and the rest, whose names I did not gather.

The way started through the crowded Bazaar of Mirpur Khas — the 'special' town of the Mirs of Sind, who ruled the country before the British came. Driving through these Bazaars is a nightmare for those not used to it — everybody a jay-walker, all across the road, bullock carts, donkeys and camels, ditto — then through the outskirts where we saw painted ladies lounging outside their lodgings, a 'Red Light' district, it seems, and some of the principal attractions distinctly attractive too.

After about thirty miles we were met by the son, Nawabsadar Amiralia Khan, in his Jeep — a young country gentleman dressed in an excellent English suit, with his Muslim furry cap above. After greetings, we went ahead and now, every hundred yards or so, we saw horsemen on gaily comparisoned steeds, like statues along by the road. Each one in turn filed in behind us until we had a mounted escort a hundred strong trotting behind us at the fast Sindi trot or 'punt', the horse moves with very quick short steps while the rider sits immobile upon it. These horses have to be specially trained, and I much admired the good horsemanship of their riders — none of that beating and tugging which is the practice of common Gharry-wallahs in towns. These were proud horsemen on their own horses, lesser land-owners who had come out specially to meet us, and 450 rode along in a disciplined body. We were quite thrilled to look back and see them accompanying us, with their picturesque coloured numdas, plumes and colours on their horse; the flowing coloured clothes and turbans made a sight to see.

We drove through mango groves up to a great arched gate with the colourful local population waiting to greet us. Through that there was the Nawab's own bodyguard drawn up to salute us — all ex-soldiers, now his retainers, with rifles and bayonets complete. They presented arms smartly, Sam Ridley took the salute and the old Nawab and his brother came out to greet us.

We were led into a big old bungalow, which dates back to 18th century. Inside there was a long veranda with fine Persian carpets and a well furnished drawing-room where we sat with our hosts.

Luncheon was of ten courses, served by neatly dressed servants in proper white uniforms — not always the case, with these rich country folk, who often allow their servants to go around in any old clothes. The food excellent and not too rich or greasy for our Western stomachs. The old Nawab and his brother had departed to say their prayers, it being Friday (the Muslim Sabbath).

Of the younger men who entertained us, half had recently been travelling in Europe and Britain — others were to go to America next year, to California University, returning and going through Europe as a sort of Grand Tour. They were much preoccupied with how to get seats at the Coronation next year (we envied them the means to go there at will) and showed us a wonderful achkan, or dress coat of frock-coat length, in black velvet lined with silk and the finest heavy gold facings and epaulettes encrusting it. We begged them to wear it at the Coronation, which seemed to surprise them, but we assured them that it would be welcomed as a compliment to the Queen, showing from what far countries gentlefolk had come to see her crowned and pointed out that ordinary

Crags on the way to Ziarat.

Western dress is dull and ordinary, while every Englishman who is entitled to it will be wearing rich dress-ceremonial uniforms — Field Marshals, Admirals, Dukes, Bishops and the like. This is their Sindi traditional dress, which they used to wear in the old days as rulers of this country.

During lunch they played an excellent radio and, to our joy, we heard a relay of the Christmas link-up throughout the world and carols from King's Choir at Cambridge — and then, what we had missed through not having a radio of our own, the Christmas message from our own Queen. The Nawabsadah had listened to it the night before, but turned it on again for our benefit. We all rose to attention to the strains of God Save the Queen; and they hushed their servants to let us hear the message. It came through so clearly and that sincere young voice spoke forth such a message of devotion, duty and goodwill; well, I think some of us were moved almost to tears — I fancy April was, for one.

After lunch there were some films of previous parties and entertainments, taken by our hosts with their cine-camera. They said they would have staged a sort of village fair and wrestling for us, only they were in mourning for a young girl who had died, a young sister. Finally, they grouped us on the terrace, took a photograph of us and hosts, and then we had to go.

The military fell in; the hosts said goodbye, and Ridley took the salute (he is the Revenue Commissioner for this Province, second only to the Governor, one of the old I.C.S. asked to stay on by the Pakistanis).

The mounted horsemen fell in behind, while we smiled and waved to them and the various other lesser folk gathered to see us off. I particularly admired the leading horseman; lean and wiry, with keen very sharp-cut features as he sat absolutely still on his horse while it paced along at speed with those quick bird-like steps of the Sindi punt — his coloured reins held quietly but firmly, a hand of authority raised to restrain any other horseman who drew too far ahead. They seemed like mounted statues in motion, so to speak, with baggy trousers and neat waisted coat, full turbans and neatly cut beards. As we turned onto the canal road, he halted the cortège and we waved mutual farewells through the windows of the speeding car.

Quetta

I had almost forgotten how vastly majestic and awe-inspiring these great barren crags can be — the brown of stags' antlers in shadow and liquid gold in sunshine and the evening makes them purply-blue:

Quetta market.

Quetta hills.

and I remember when we lived here in 1940, how the autumn sunset used to turn them a lurid salmon pink (tinned variety). I have already wasted a lot of paper trying to make crayon sketches of their majesties, but fear I've failed utterly. I have also been sketching a most beautiful mosque which is being built for the Policemen. It has one large and two small most *lovely* domes, ribbed with lotus petals at the base. Thro' it we have met a most delightful and 'moti' Punjabi Officer-in-Charge, from whom we asked permission to come into the police grounds and sketch. He says they transported the best Punjabi workmen they could find to build for them and that each man of the Force has already given a whole month's pay towards the making — but as it is not yet finished, they will all now have to give another month's pay; rather an example to Christians, don't you think? But mosques, which always fascinate me, are most difficult to draw, I find — the domes are so very subtle in shape. I remember spending many many hours in Lahore making a sketch of the huge

Police mosque, Quetta.

one there; it has zig-zag stripes going around the domes, if you remember, and whenever we go to Hala, which is quite often, I do yet another view of the blue-tiled mosque there.

Quetta is cold — beautifully *cold* (and my face cream is no longer oil). The skies are very blue and the great clouds a glistening white and yesterday, when we arrived from Sukkur (where the heat is so intense that I could neither sleep nor rest), the winds here are *icy* and we had fires made in both sitting-room and bedroom, hot-water bottles put in the beds and my big fur coat unpacked — such a contrast within ten hours. Previously I had only come up the Bolan Pass by train and so was thrilled to motor now. Geoffrey drove so that I could just look, but it was not such steep going as coming from the Punjab up to Fort Munroe, and the road was nearly twice as wide. We met all kinds of entrancing people with camels and Powinda gypsies with their fierce crop-eared dogs and, later on, miners who were getting coal from little holes in the mountain sides.

I must tell you about the Kabul camel man. You know the almost everlasting flat bit of desert between Jacobabad and Sibi, parallel to the railway, which is just desert for miles and miles and MILES and only mirages of lakes and islands break the almost hypnotic monotony? (I love mirages; the last bit of magic left in the world.) Far ahead we saw a lone figure on the road who waved frantically — I stopped the car and he got in, Sekhander Khan, our six-foot Pathan bearer, and Hassan the Driver looking very uppish as the jungli Pathan-type sat between them, his heavily nailed shoes in his hand. He said he was taking camels back to Kabul but they were along the road; so on we sped till a horsemen came in sight. The Pathan then let out the most piercing 'YIPPEE' yell, just behind my head and we all nearly jumped thro' the roof. By the time I had stopped, the horse had gone well into the distance but the jungli leaped out, our men threw his shoes into the road after him and by much tooting of the horn the horseman came back at a gallop, turned the animal on two legs to stop and our Pathan mounted behind his pal who had presumably come out to look for him. Much further along the road we passed a herd of camels — and that yell is still with me!

In spite of the cold the Hotel gardens are covered with roses and more roses, pansies, verbena, cornflower, columbine, laburnam and *more* roses. There are some great crimson beauties that turn purple when they are nearly over and in the cascades of flowering creeper outside the veranda window small and strong birds sing beautifully. The mali, who looks a Mongolian type, has just brought me in two bowls of flowers arranged in his best fashion. The *pièce de résistance* is a circle of orange-yellow poppies with three bright 'coolie pink' cabbage roses in the centre. He has put the vase against a Russian-red teapot that caught my fancy in the bazaar — colourful is a mild description! By the way, there are hundreds of these teapots in every china shop and all made in Japan — in fact Japan seems to have already captured the Quetta market.

Blanche

Pariah dog.

Fishing dhow.

I have adopted Blanche the white pariah lady; she comes bounding and smiling when I call her, which is very sweet. And if she is extra pleased she waves her tail, not, as you might imagine, from side to side or even up and down; but round and round and round like a clockwork toy — it is too odd!

She is elegantly shaped like a greyhound and pure creamy white all over except for her black nose and beautiful hazel eyes. Who previously fed her I cannot think, but now every evening she comes to me for a plateful of bones and scraps and then walks over to the mali-pond for a drink of nice muddy water. Then she is all set for an evening of vigorous barking and proceeds to rush out at every other animal in sight and shout at the top of her voice in a very possessive manner.

By the Tombs of the Mirs

Hyderabad, Sind

We have just come down from Quetta, in Baluchistan — where we once lived in 1940 when Geoffrey was a Mountain Gunner — which is surrounded by some of the highest mountains in the world. G. has a refugee town to plan and there is a lot of interesting work entailed, if only he has the time. We had quite a gay time, as the Political Agent and his wife and the Revenue Commissioners are English and old friends and we met quite a few more. The bazaar is a fascinating place and it is good to see the very pale skins and light eyes of the Afghans. The children all seem to have pinky cheeks and some people looked quite Mongolian; they had come from Turkestan — a motley collection which fascinated me greatly and I have made quite a lot of sketches. On the way back it was even more interesting to come *down* the Bolan Pass than to go up. It is nearly as famous as the Khyber (Robert's army wound its weary way up there to Kandahar)

The Tombs of the Mirs.

and much more spectacular. It takes over three hours to come winding down in a car and the huge ranges of rock have been so twisted in some pre-historic upheaval that the strata make the most fantastic patterns and shapes, like nothing else in the world. Have I said no grass — no trees — grow anywhere? It is macabre and unreal. When at last down in the valleys we met the tribes, their hundreds of camels all strung out one behind the other, tied tail to nose. Babies, goats, beds, hens and ancients up aloft. Men and women walking alongside and as interested in us as we in them — so must Abraham and his tribe have looked; nothing changes. The woman wear long dark-red robes embroidered with bits of mirror-glass across the yoke, so that they flash in the sun, like breastplates. Long veils are put over their braided hair and they have huge silver ear-rings like domes, with jingles at the edge. As soon as the mountains warm up and the icy winds cease — in fact Spring comes — these nomads leave the plains. They live in low black-hair tents, rounded over the top like an igloo — and with them they have their huge and very fierce biscuit-coloured dogs and they crop the dogs' ears, to make them fiercer they say. When the dogs see a car they come roaring and growling their hair bristling, in an angry charge, and would no doubt tear any stranger to pieces.

Now we are back in Sukkur for two days, staying in the 'Royal suite' of the Circuit House, which looks onto the nearly-two-mile-wide Indus, across lawns and flowers and trees. But in spite of these the days are so *hot* that we cannot with any comfort go out after 8.30 a.m. or before 5.30 p.m. So I sit writing letters. Sukkur is about 200 miles from Hyderabad and across the river is built the great Lloyd Barrage.

Constructed by the British in the 1920s it has brought water, food and prosperity to much of the Sind Desert and yet you probably have never even heard of it — but if the Americans had done it, the Barrage would be world famous! It is stretching away from this bank and as the rounded arches murge into a blur the end is a pin-point. The fishing folk of Sukkur live in their great wooden boats, shaped like wooden shoes and now line the river bank with the hundreds of water buffaloes who wallow the day through. Some of the smaller boats have cormorants and grey herons chained to an outrigger, to do the fishing, as do the Chinese. The river has quite a few little islands scattered about — one is entirely encircled by a mud fort, a relic of 100 years ago — but is still garrisoned. Another is covered with trees and in the groves were white marble Hindu temples and sacred peacocks. We once, in 1944 I think, visited the isle and saw the peacocks dancing — stamping and furling their tails like fans, as they courted the dull hens.

Tomorrow, before sunrise, we leave for Hyderabad, so that some of the 200 miles will be done in the coolth. The roads are so shocking in Lower Sind that one wastes a great deal of time and there are also the great herds of goats, camels, donkeys and, above all, bone-headed humans who make hazards every mile or so on the narrow strip of tarmac. At the edges is sand with great hollows and rifts which are sometimes covered with rushes for miles to keep the dust down — but of course the fine sandy dust gets into everything, even locked suitcases. I always do nearly all the driving, as G. likes to sit and think and possibly sleep, and our Servants (the Bearer and Driver who never drives but changes tyres and polishes!) sit behind us and then behind that comes the luggage which always seems to be mountainous. Tell Tedda it was a real thrill for me to take the wheel up and down the pass — I really *like* being the chauffeuse.

Our two cats, Shamus and Friday, and beautiful Blanche, the white and elegant pariah bitch who guards the house, and no doubt the fat cross-eyed Cook and the Hamal (dusting boy) Akbar, and Syed Mohammed the Orderly, plus an enormous pile of letters I hope, will be awaiting us. I feel we have been out of the world a long time, tho' it is only two weeks.

Hyderabad, Sind

How much I agree with your ideas of motoring — can't think of anything I should like better than to be *with you;* I just ache for green England as well as my loved friends, but you mustn't give me too much sympathy for living here. I am doing very well. I have not yet been ill — really ill I mean — and for Geoffrey this is the chance of a lifetime and one that *any* architect in the world must long for [the siting of the new capital], the only trouble is that he can't move quickly enough. The two — no THREE — Ministers his work comes under *never* get together or agree upon anything and he must have some official approval before he can plan and design a great capital city. To satisfy someone or other, we went off on Sunday in the Chevrolet station-wagon to look at what is known as the 'Lake Site' — tho' there is no lake within many miles or will be for years, but canals are being run that way and eventually a great area of land the Karachi side of Tatta will be under water. Among others, Sam Ridley wanted the capital to be put there. Anyway, out we went, leaving before the hot, about 6.30 a.m., and taking the Driver (who is never allowed to drive) and two Orderlies, all of them Pathans and tough. Our first trouble was the little fan-wheel that drives the batteries — that went phut — but fortunately we stopped at a big P.W.D. workshop which repairs the giant dragline things that make canals and within an hour we had a new one fitted. In the meanwhile G. and I went about half a mile and wallowed in the shallow Indus water that was overflowing into some fields, so that was a pleasant way of waiting.

Then came the fun. Still with me driving we plunged off the main road and took the tracks across the desert, to get to the 'lakes'. It was frightful going and if the car hadn't been so high off the ground we should never have got across. Up nullahs and down wadis and across stony ridges we went — you know the kind of country. Then we had lunch under the only tree for miles. The three men had brought their lunch as instructed but *no* water, so we gave them half of our tea and water; a thing I hadn't counted on. You can imagine what came next — we got *stuck* utterly with the wheels bogged in sand, the axles on a ridge and the car at an angle. All because during one of the 'levelling operations' which they are quite used to — the men with spade, powrah and pickaxe clear the tracks for the car — G. beckoned me forward to come gingerly onto the little path made for the car — and then Hassan, silly fool, suddenly rushed forward to move just one little bit of something and I thought he was practically under the front wheels and having yelled 'Hassan!', then let the car slip sideways — and we got caught. I suppose it was better than going over him but it took *two* solid hours under that blazing early-afternoon sun before the car could move again. There just weren't any stones near to make any kind of platform and the two jacks were only good for a six-inch move — and having given our water away at lunch-time, G. and the three men had to work becoming thirstier

Rhori at the Indus.

112

and thirstier. I can quite see how men go mad for lack of water in quite a short time. We discovered some flat stones about a quarter of a mile away — big heavy slabs — and the four of them carried some on their shoulders to the car, then back again. It was quite dreadful to see them so utterly exhausted. One oldish man could hardly stand up and seemed very ill, but we got out — backwards — and then had to go a long way round on the high ridges. Once more we got bogged in sand but that was only a matter of putting branches under the wheels and eventually we made Jhimpir Station and rushed to the station taps — and tho' the water tasted warm and a bit of old train (I thought) it was marvellous. Later we rested in the horrid dirty little waiting-room and sat naked under the tap of warm water and that was marvellous too. And then came the fun of getting out of Jhimpir, with the only cutcha track washed away and not even a Jeep could have tackled that. The result was we arrived back here about 7 p.m. after a most tiring day, I having driven 120 miles and our opinion of the so-called Lake Site is *not* printable! There isn't anywhere to build a decent capital, anyway.

Rhori.

The hyenas

January, 1953

This morning before breakfast, we motored out to the fishing village near the Flying Boat Base. It is quite large and has some houses of real brick among the usual hovels of baked mud and rushes, while cows and goats, hens, ducks and buffaloes give an air of prosperity. But we hear they have no well and the women must go over a mile away for fresh water, bringing it back in huge earthenware chattis which they balance on their heads as they walk in stately procession like a Greek frieze.

The fishing boats were all drawn up on the flat beaches and beyond were miles of lonely sand-dunes lashed with sea and spray.

After we had been stared at by a rapidly increasing crowd of young and old, the Headman came forward and invited us to look at his TIGERS! Utterly mystified we followed, to see a low brick-built shed, barred at the one open end; and from it glared and snarled a very angry hyena. It was like an enormous dog with tawny bristling mane and hind quarters striped in black. Deep lion-like grunts came from its throat as it bared its long yellow fangs. In a nearby pit, staked with wires and pegged under a fishing net was another even larger. It was practically dead. The night before these fishermen had caught these huge hyenas out on the dunes when the brutes had come sneaking in to prey on the goats and calves; and it can have been no easy feat, as hyenas are strong and ferocious.

In answer to the Headman's questions as to what he should now do with them we told him to borrow a gun from the Air Force and quickly put the 'Tigers' out of their obvious misery.

You must own that we meet with very unexpected sights before breakfast!

Old Arloo, stall and infant son.

Old Arloo

Hyderabad

I must tell you the tale of Old Arloo, or, in English, 'Old Potato'. He had a little fruit and sweet-potato stall outside the shanty tea-shops which fringe the gardens of the big English hotel in which we stay. Every evening at sundown when we came out of our palatial-looking abode to feed the monkeys and the little bear, old Arloo, supported by his twelve-year-old son, sold us pounds of this and that for the chattering monkeys. Sometimes another, very young, Arloo, dressed in a tiny shirt and red shoes on his minute feet, would be sitting amongst the weights and balances and be playing with the smooth stone that did duty for a half-pound weight. After we had known him for a few weeks, we noticed he sold the aloos only, saying that fruit was too dear and that he could make no profit, and we were sorry to see him so depressed and missed the cheery toothless smile he usually turned upon us. Then one evening he asked G. if he could find him a job as he could no longer feed his poor little family. And so we have brought him up here to Hyderabad as an Office Peon. His face, as G. gave him an official letter of appointment, was spread with a beatific smile of utter incredulity — out of the blue his prayers were answered!

The monkeys of Karachi

I have been feeding the monkeys — and some of their owners! They sit patiently awaiting me on a pile of rubble and stones by the side of a little native 'hotel'. I say that I will come when the sun is setting because the monkey people do not understand time and anyway have no watches tucked away in the bag of needments that each carries over his shoulder.

The men and boys sit on their heels chatting and keeping their monkeys from fighting each other. They wear earth-stained shirts and skirts that were once white or brightly coloured but are now just tones of greyish brown. Each has a pair of monkeys on strings attached to heavy collars; and the collars have worn away the hair on the tiny thin necks, so that pale wrinkled skin shews through. Some of the animals are decked out in tawdry red skirts and jackets and one possesses a little hat that its owner pulls from the jumbled mass of clothes, bowls, drums and sticks that he keeps in his bag. Some of them are big bad-tempered old males who fill their pouches to over-flowing in a most ill-mannered fashion, and some are tiny and gentle ladies who will put one bird-like and fragile hand in mine while with the other they hold the pieces of apple or orange that I give them. They chatter and give shrill cries but their eyes look baffled and sorrowful and wring my heart with pity.

Sometimes a baby Himalayan bear is brought along too. She is about three feet high and has a ring through one nostril. She is gentle as a kitten and squeals with joy when we give her a bowl of warm milk, bought from the 'hotel' behind us.

Old Arloo's stall of fruit and sweet potatoes does a brisker trade at sundown than at any other time of the day and the stone that represents a 1 lb. weight is in constant demand. The Sweeper's children who always line the front row of spectators are like little monkeys themselves and, as I peel oranges, they too stand with mouths open waiting for me to pop in a segment. The tiny girls have ear-rings — and so have the lady monkeys!

When the animals have eaten their fill and when the owners have all received four annas each from us, the crowd, which by this time is two or three deep, disperses and the monkeys are hoisted on to their owners' shoulders. 'Cul ana' — 'Come back tomorrow' — we tell them and at tomorrow's sunset they will all be there again.

Young Sindi girl.

Locusts

Karachi, January, 1953

This mid-afternoon, low in the sky across the Maidan, we saw a dark brown cloud, miles in width, coming up from the distant country; and as it is not the season for rain it could only mean locusts.

At first they were only sparse numbers fluttering against the blue sky in a helpless manner — but heralds of millions.

Children ran out to try and knock them down as they wavered like toy aeroplanes about four inches long; within less than half an hour they were thick around us and beat against the closed windows of the car. The sky became one whirring mass of winged bodies and all we could see, looking towards the Harbour, was the fire of the sun shimmering through the reddish haze of the tightly-packed winged bodies. Quickly, the sand-dunes, the immediate ground before us and then the light were blotted out with the suddenness of an eclipse; darkness came while the sun was still high. The papery whisper of millions of wings was part of the unrestrained horror that had descended from a clear sky. Every tree near us had a creeping carpet of the ravenous plague clinging to it and was stripped naked; but fortunately the wind came from the land, and the masses moved towards the Arabian Sea; at one point the westering sunlight caught their wings so that we saw no longer the brown cloud of bodies but instead a gently fluttering snowstorm like a stage effect. Coming back, we watched the locals bundling fallen locusts into the hems of their shirts, scarves, unwound puggarees and anything handy. Fried locusts are reckoned a *great* delicacy!

Alphonso

Today, as we came back from our early morning walk on the Maidan, we heard a small boy singing to a white pigeon which he held between his hands. G. asked him what he was going to do with it and he replied 'Eat it — but you may have it for a rupee.' This, of course, was too much for us and in half a minute I was carrying the pigeon and the small boy was dancing off with a jingle in his pocket.

It was a bedraggled bird and I planned to let it fly from our high veranda; but it took one look at the great outside, then turned and walked sedately into the sitting-room and perched on the back of a chair! I believe it wants to stay and we have bought millet and other little seeds and made a place on top of the wardrobe, where it sits on one leg and then on t'other; but not often on both at once. G. has christened it Alphonso.

Alphonso.

Before the sun has really broken through the winter mists on the Maidan our chota hazri arrives — tea and two yellow apples. At this signal, Alphonso, who all night has been folded up on the edge of the high cupboard, stands. First easing one wing to full stretch and then the other, he flutters wildly, gyrating as he gathers speed, so that within a few seconds he is just a soft white blur of beating sounds; this continues quite a while before the momentum slackens, the dust settles and a few downy feathers descend to the blue carpet below. The nice English Steward has lent us a large parrot-cage, which now stands on top of the cupboard and Alphonso sometimes sits in it — but not often; though the door is ever open so that he need not feel frustrated.

Last night Alphonso seemed to have bad dreams, and purred and gurgled a lot; and this morning has fluttered onto the blades of the ceiling fan. I switched it on very slowly and gave him a ride, which he seemed to enjoy. Now he is asleep on the perch in the parrot-cage and looks very huffy. He can get out quite well, but doesn't want to; he regards the cage as a place of safe retreat. He is becoming very uppity and smacks at us with his wings and purrs angrily. The room Sweeper, who has a lot of pigeons and should know, says Alphonso is a female and longs for a husband! Shall he bring one? I say 'Yes' and that I will come to see his birds and choose a pretty one.

Before sundown, I went across to a forgotten garden and met the jolly Sweeper and all his brood of infants and his wife and his old mother enjoying the sharp cool of the evening. We all stood watching the white pigeons as they came to their nests in a wooden box hung on the garden wall. With great care we decided on a husband for Alphonso — a pure white beauty with black eyes and coral feet — and brought him back to the parrot-cage.

At first, so that they might become acquainted gradually, we kept the husband in the cage and let Alphonso walk about outside. When (s)he didn't seem particulouarly overjoyed to see the new arrival we put it down to shyness. After a while we put them together and waited for a happy cooing — but *whang!* they beat each other with hard outstretched wings and positively roared with anger. I hastily withdrew Alphonso. The Sweeper, whom we again called in, pointed out that all husbands and wives quarrelled, and why shouldn't pigeons? We again felt he should know.

During the night, one sat in the cage and one without, both throwing millet seeds all over the floor in a deliberate and angry manner. This morning, the denouement has come. When I put them again together in the cage they really fought like fury, roaring and gobbling and beating each other in abandoned rage. The truth is — but you have guessed it — they are both MALES! So we have taken them both to the pigeon garden and released them. Gone are my dreams of starting a colombier; and the last I saw was Alphonso strutting up and down the roof of old pink tiles with a scornful look in his knowing eyes.

The Ritz Hotel

Hyderabad, Sind

How amused Caesar Ritz would be to see this extraordinary little place perpetuating his memory! This morning I feel that I have been sleeping on paving stones all night and I ache in every bone. The bed is a solid wooden platform and the mattress just a two-inch thickness of Sindi cotton; the pillows seem to be stuffed with hard knobs. Who slept with a stone for his pillow? Daniel? But he had visions to comfort him. Apart from the bed and a chair, there is no more furniture in the little white-washed room; Pakistani ladies have only scarves and tunics to put away in neatly folded squares and the shallow niches in the walls are designed for this purpose.

As a bathroom, there is a small 3 ft. by 5 ft. cell with a handbasin and taps, one of which works. There is also a tiny shower but when it is on all the water runs through to the bedroom and makes a lake on the floor, so that I have to rush in and snatch up my shoes which line one wall in a neat row. Across one side of the cell is a small platform for the oriental W.C.; a call from nature entails squatting over a waisted porcelain trough and a spouted can filled with water takes the place of the Western 'bumf'. Then, miracle of miracles, there is a perfect flush cistern overhead, but once the 'pull' has operated, the outside open drain takes care of the rest, just below our open window. It is mediaeval, but not so much as some I have patronised in the past — that is another story!

The Beggars

Hyderabad

I have just escaped from a hoard of filthy ragged beggars — women, young boys, small children and minute babies. I was walking down the little main street of the bazaar, when this cluster of wretched humanity fastened upon me like flies; and having distributed all my change to one woman, before I was aware of the rest of the tribe, I fled ignominiously. But at the next corner came another group of equal filth and misery, who, seeing I had given money to the first lot, made a whining procession after me; the babies cried piteously — pinched for the effect I am sure — the children pushed their grasping little hands into my face and the mothers displayed their rags and tatters and howled for clothes. In the face of this tribe of want and woe I could do nothing and so decided to walk in a slow and determined manner, looking neither to right or to left until I have arrived at the Ritz.

Sindi milkman.

The Bungalow

Hyderabad

This bungalow is built on a hard stony ridge of desert. The ridge reflects the heat like a burning-glass and the hot winds blow dust all over the verandas and through into the living-rooms so that absolutely everything has a coating of fine dust. It gets into the cupboards and

Derelict mosque, Sind desert.

drawers and of course all over the furniture and the curtains. Sekander Khan and Akbar dust the whole house through three and four times a day.

When we first came here, there seemed to be no green thing to soften this barrack-like house; but since Christmas we have had two small patches of grass laid on either side of the veranda door. They are made from cut squares of turf, brought on the backs of little sad-eyed donkeys. The Mali and his two water-men first arranged bricks endwise, so that a saw-toothed edge divides the grass from the desert; then he planted marigolds and cosmos at even intervals in a narrow border, and now he is trying to grow G's name in what he calls 'Lal garse' or Red Grass, a two-inch high plant with tiny reddish-coloured leaves which these Muslims love for their formal gardens.

Because water is so precious, G. has constructed a little canal from the bathroom outlets and the bathwater, instead of vanishing Heaven-knows-where, now comes coursing down the canal to the flower-bed under the side windows. That bed has taken a great deal of making. Pick handles have been broken regularly as G., for morning exercise and accompanied by our Driver and two Orderlies, has laboured for over three weeks hacking out the small rocks and concrete-like sand of the ridge. When the long trough was about four feet deep, many loads of earth and loam were brought by bullock-cart to fill it. The Bullocky, as we would say in Australia, dressed in a bright red turban and striped shirt, came with a heavy wooden-wheeled cart and it was quite delightful to hear him coaxing his oxen to turn and spill out the loads 'Now Baby — here — here'. 'Up Old One, this side, come — come'. So we hope to have quick growing papayas (paw-paws to you) against a dark background of castor oil plants. You realise that we cannot wait for the slow-growing plants and must have something that will cover and shade within a month or two. Papayas, as you know, are excellent eating, though I cannot say the same about the castor oils!

We seem to have imbued Hassan the Driver with ideas about plants for the garden and, to our consternation, on the day we had lunch with H.E. the Governor and his wife, we found that Hassan had spent his waiting time in collecting specimens from the Circuit House garden and proudly produced eight small eucalyptus saplings when we got into the car! The Head Mali was a friend of his he told us — Hassan has more friends than anyone I have ever known, and even in the most unlikely desert places, pals come rushing towards him with open arms; he certainly has the sweetest nature and smile you can imagine. So now we hope that the Blue Gums will take firm root and be a reminder of our dear Australia!

Flowers

This morning I have arranged the flowers, using yesterday's water; yesterday there was plenty of water, but no fresh flowers. The thin little Mali who wears a round black hat and special sleeveless mali coat, gives me a gentle smile as he brings marigolds of pale and deep gold, orange-flecked cannas, tiny velvety-brown daisies and some black-centred sunflowers. These are for the dining-room and go in the crude lemon-yellow vase that the village potter of Hala made. I have to disentangle all these glorious yellows from the pink, white and cherry petunias and the blue and purple cornflowers he adds to the bunch before I can dress up the white strap-work china bowl. It is Spode and very old and travels wherever I do. Against the cool pale-blue walls of the sitting-room the petunias all merge in tone and make a glow of mauve, casting grey-blue shadows on the wall behind. What an infinite pleasure these colours give me!

Shamus-the-cat's-child lies curled in baby sleep on the Kashmir carpet that is embroidered all over in pale greys and pinks and occasional small touches of indigo and raspberry red. It is very beautiful — and so is Shamus, except for his rather too-long back legs; but all native cats seem to be that shape.

Coolies

In Karachi

This evening, as we had much small shopping to do before returning to Hyderabad, we walked down to the cobbled streets that are the Borhi Bazaar of Karachi (the Borhis are the Mohammedan hardware merchants and wear delightful little muslin hats and long black beards). The alleys are very narrow and the shops sometimes just large boxes big enough to hold a man and his wares; sometimes they are good-sized stores. But whatever the sizes, they are always stacked brimful, the doorsteps and outside walls festooned with merchandise, so that one wonders how they ever 'shut shop' at all, and how long next morning it takes again to hang out the bird-cages, hose-pipes and multiples of this and that.

Coolies help with the shopping.

On my list was 'Oven for Rozario, Alarum Clock, Cat's Saucers, Buckets, Lanterns, Small Tray, Coffee-Pot, Rope'. No sooner were we spotted as prospective purchasers than a small boy darted up, then another, then an aged man and a youth or two, and by the time we had pushed our way into the very narrow hardware shop, its entrance was besieged. Coolies with large rush baskets begged to carry our wares. Each and every tried to catch our attention; 'Sahib, I first coolie' — 'Mem-sahib, I best coolie' — and, of course, the inevitable 'No mamma, no pappa, give baksheesh' from some of the more aged. They don't seem to have a clue to the meaning — it is just a beggars' cry and old men will wail that they have no parents to support them!

When we had carefully tested the lamps, measured the tin oven with its glass door — Rozario will put it over the charcoal fire and cook all kinds of good things, I hope — had a long argument as to the merits of china, aluminium or enamel for cat's dishes, and bought several oddments that were not on the list, the chatter of the coolies outside, backed by an interested crowd of loafers, was simply deafening. Hearing all the pleading voices outside, I was sorry that so many poor creatures must be disappointed. But not Geoffrey! With the wisdom of Solomon, he let each man and boy carry something, however small, until they ceased to grab and gave way to laughter.

At the main street a lad was sent off to bring a taxi while the rest waited on the kerb, each with his charge in hand. And when the taxi pulled up we were amused to see the unwashed and tattered coolie, not standing on the running-board but sitting in the back seat and riding proudly and in great state. Possibly it was the first time he had ever been in a taxi and he was making the most of it! Then came the great moment of payment and thin brown hands stretched eagerly for a few annas — and to judge by the profound salaams we received from the jolly fellows as we drove off, G. had grossly overpaid them. Unfortunately, when we got back to the hotel, the lift-boy dropped the alarum clock, but even that catastrophe couldn't mar the fun of our shopping.

Pi-dogs

Hyderabad, Sind

Almost every morning after breakfast and after I have inspected the contents of the refrigerator, the cleanliness or otherwise of the kitchen and given orders for the day, I sit down with my typewriter and my Oxford Dictionary (because as you probably know from much past experience, I just *can't* spell) and I write letters. So I have done this morning, but I don't seem to be able to concentrate — a state that I can only put down to LACK OF SLEEP. The pi-dogs have kept us awake practically all night as they barked and quarrelled and fought, and this morning both G. and I feel wrecks. 'Pi-dog' is a corruption of Pariah Dog and I suppose the species has existed for thousands of years. They are rather beautiful to look at, shaped like small greyhounds with short fine coats and tails that curl like a spring. In colour they are usually white or foxy red or biscuit and they have sweet mild eyes of amber or hazel. By day they are timid and cowed and with the sunrise most of them go to their holes which they dig in the sand and sleep. But with the dusk they emerge and hungrily search for food off rubbish piles, carrion, or sit at a respectful distance from the humans in tea-shops, hoping for a scrap of chapatti to be thrown them.

Some are semi-domesticated and, when on their own territory, kept as watch-dogs by the village people and have the fierceness of lions. It is only prudent to arm oneself with large stones if passing one of the mud villages because when half a dozen half-starved pi-dogs rush out one thing only will control them — a shower of stones. We throw to frighten them, never intending to make a direct hit, but the native will find the protruding ribs and skeleton flanks of a pi-dog irresistible and aims to hurt. If a dog can be found in a sound sleep, all the better for his aim — and the wild screaming of the poor things makes me miserable. We find that the mere action of bending down for a pretence stone good enough in most cases, and off they go. Blanche, Boy, her pale-reddish brother, and old Three-and-a-half-legs (because one thigh is dislocated and he goes hoppity) have all accepted us, are fed twice a day with bones and scraps and love having their heads patted and adore being taken with us on our evening walk, just like real dogs; but as soon as we leave the environs of this colony and get towards Jacob's Tank and the collection of mud huts behind a barricade of thorn, where two or three families have their dwelling, Blanche's tail turns down and she turns for home; Boy takes a little longer to trot off and I never see old Three-legs vanish — but he just isn't there. You see, it is the village-dogs' territory and they come roaring out ready to chew up any trespasser, canine or human.

On the other hand, here outside our bungalow, these Pis of ours create hell's-own-delight by barking at and attacking any and every other dog they see passing. Some of the tribes that pass with their camels have their watch-dogs on leads; this seems to infuriate ours more than usual and the noise they make as these harmless and cowed animals pass is incredible. By night all this is ten times as bad, because the desert dogs seem to hunt in packs and come rushing through our compound in dozens and half-dozens attacking and being attacked, being bitten and biting until the night is a bedlam.

Pi-dogs and bear.

Hyderabad Dhobi

Our washerman in Hyderabad is a smiling well-built Hindu. When we first arrived, there were at least three Dhobis waiting to present their credentials. One by one they brought out tattered envelopes containing dog-eared chittis for G. to inspect; and they stood in a small row as he read through these old letters with forgotten names and addresses, extolling the unique skill of each man. Then suddenly we came to a letter dated 1940 and headed with a familiar number in the Mall — it was our own chit, recommending most highly this washerman who never beat on stone or tore with pointed irons or 'lost' socks and handkerchiefs in the wash, and so of course we *had* to have him!

The Bearer announces him, 'Dhobi is here, Mem-sahib', and then goes to the wicker clothes baskets in our two bathrooms and fishes out all that we wore and used yesterday. I sit with pencil and notebook and make a list with the Dhobi solemnly counting and the Bearer re-counting, and all is bundled up and taken away on a bicycle by this happily smiling man.

The Dhobi ghats are on the ridge by the old bungalow we used to have. I have in the past so often listened in the greyness of early morning to the 'Whang-Whang' as the nearly-naked little brown men, expelling each breath with the action of their arms, beat holes into and buttons off so many shirts and trousers, while their small sons gathered stones to roll among the handfuls of handkerchiefs and collars! But in 1940 we testified that this particular man did not '*beat* or tear', and when the quick sundown comes he is again in the house, his hands holding a carefully folded bundle in a piece of white cloth and my blouses and dresses displayed on a home-made hanger of twig; and I know he has used the long thorns of the barbul-tree to pin out his washing on the clothes-line under the trees and that his young daughter has done all the careful ironing which he displays with such assurance. Has he not our chit, written thirteen years ago, to say how good he is — and can we doubt our own words?

The Sooter-Booter

Hyderabad, January, 1953

Sekander Khan is adamant and is almost choking with indignation through his protruding front teeth. He will *not* have Syed Mohammed the new Hamal in the house! There has been a bitter quarrel and he refers to Syed Mohammed as a 'Sooter-Booter'. We ask what the name means and are told that it is a new-fashioned young man who wears suits and boots (ugh!) instead of the old-fashioned baggy trousers and long shirt and puggaree. Now, Syed Mohammed is a tough-looking young Pathan who has been fighting against the Hindus up in Kashmir and, though he usually wears the shalwar trousers and long shirt of the tribesman, this day he had European trousers and a cast-off sports jackets of Geoffrey's and wore laced-up shoes instead of the sandals called chapplies. Anyway, with his shining black hair worn in a long bob under his Jinnah hat he probably looks too handsome and cocky to be controlled by old Sekander Khan — and so — *out!* We must find some other job for this Sooter-Booter. I shall suggest that toothless Arloo, who says he was a Sahib's Bearer *once*, take Syed's place.

January 25th — later

Alas! that arrangement did not last long. On the second morning, Arloo came late, buoyant and reckless in sinful sloth. There was an understandable quarrel and remarks were bitter, and, unfortunately, mainly concerned with TEETH. Sekander Khan has a rush of buck fangs and in Arloo's mouth there is a solitary spike. Now we shall have to find some other job for Arloo — Oh dear!

Sekander Khan and the Sooter-Booter.

Famine on a starving horse

19th February, 1953

Today, I have seen one of the Four Horsemen — Famine on a starving horse. This was an emaciated woman — old or young I couldn't tell — seated on the skeleton of a white horse. It neither hastened nor halted, but kept the same walking pace, head bowed.

The woman sat straight as a ram-rod, her tattered scarf about her face and the faded pink stripes of her dusty shalwar making folds over her stick-like legs and paper-thin feet. Who had put her on this wretched animal to ride to the city? Was it for help or is she the last of a prosperous family? These two haunt me.

Famine on a starving horse.

Standing in awe

I am told that the small Sweeper boy Kishin stands very much in awe of our dim-wit Akbar! He comes early in the morning and an hour later his 'Ma' arrives to help him, and together they brush the floors with short besom-like brushes or jarools, made from the waving grass heads that grow hereabouts. 'Ma' is a young and comely Marwari woman, with a dark brown glowing skin; she wears a tremendously full skirt of black and red cotton and a bright yellow shawl which she tucks into one side of the waistband; under this is a little backless but sleeved blouse. Around her neck she has a collar of ornate silver-work and in her nose a silver ring. For entering the house she comes barefoot, but outside the door are a pair of black shoes silver-embroidered, which have long turned-back toes.

Akbar started this month as a peon or office messenger, but, at his request, we have brought him into the house to be useful. He really knows nothing at all about housework, but is shown and supervised by Sekander Khan, our six-foot Pathan, and he pays him due deference as an apprentice should.

As much as Akbar pays deference with a thrill of fear to Sekander, so does Sekander pay deference to us; and we are told that the Cook, dear little Lawrence Rozario, who stands on one bare foot put across the other as he talks of roasts and stews and puddings to me, is in great awe of me — ME!

Cook and family.

Rozario

February, 1953

Our little Rozario the Cook is not happy and wishes to return to Karachi and his Goan community, and so we must let him go. It is uncanny with what swiftness the word has gone around and now *many* cooks have come asking for work. This morning we engaged one who says he used to be a Sahib's cook and his fistful of grubby chits bears out his words. When the British went, rather than hire his services to a Pakistani family, he and his brother set up a small tea-shop in the town — the kind that is known as 'Hotel' and which sells cups of tea and possibly makes chapattis. Beds are provided for the customers, who lounge at their ease in the comparatively cool and dark depths of the small shop; pet fat-tailed sheep, some painted with gaudy dabs of henna or purple ink, are probably chained to the wooden prop which holds up the awning; bits of gay tiles, small mirrors and brightly-coloured 'pin-ups' are the usual decorations around the walls and a small glass-fronted cupboard displays dummy packets of English cigarettes. Small brown-papery twists of Biris, which are the Eastern equivalent of the Woodbine, lie in neat bundles on the rickety table which also does duty as a counter.

Letter from Rozario:

Dear Madam and Sir,
Received your kind letter thanks. we are all O.K. Do not varry, we will arrange for money till your honour return to Hyd. Your honour's home & cat are O.K. we will keep them well nothing more to add
Have your servant b.regards to MemSahib & to your honour.

Yours obediently
Lawrence Rozario

The reason I engage this man is not because I particularly like the look of him — he has a ragged moustache and a bad squint — but because he has brought his family of small children with him, and it wrings my heart when he tells me the 'hotel' has failed and his children will starve. Nobody else has produced a family or such a tale, so he wins!

The storm

Hyderabad, May 20th, 1953

Here is something I have never before experienced; and it came from a clear blue sky. Forked lightning darted across the dark steel of massive cloud and then against this colossus came great spirals of whirling sand, a tremendous wind bringing them nearer and sending them higher until the whole sky was an oncoming mass of dark brown, eclipsing sun and light. It was uncanny to see the wind and yet not feel it, though my eyes were smarting from the almost invisible dust around me. Then, *whang!* the centre of the cyclone moved on and the dust rushed up, blotting out everything with the intensity of a London fog. The few spindly trees bowed almost to the ground. In less time than it takes to write, the floors are *thick* with fine sand and the furniture is covered — and it will be the work of days before things are clean again. As I looked out of a peephole window, still the pariah dogs played, dancing round each other and pretending to bite — incredible! And now, a quarter of an hour after this whirl of desolation the skies are again clear; though the forked lightning is still dancing around. We have opened windows and raised the chicks to a cool and lovely night and the servants have started to wash china and clean shelves.

Disasters

Hyderabad, 6th June, 1953

Last night, we returned here from a week in the Capital, Karachi, and were almost instantly greeted with long faces and tales of woe. Sekander Khan's house in the Frontier Province had fallen down owing to rain; his aged father-in-law was sick; his son and wife ditto, his donkeys, buffalo and goats dead, and I forget what else! The outcome was that Rs.200 were needed immediately and the Sahib and Mem-sahib must let him have it at once.

G. says that, during the war, all the troops who were at home on a week's leave and wanted it extended had houses that fell down and wild telegrams would be received to say 'Mother dangerous' or 'Father fearful'; and so with these well-tried ruses in mind, we are chary of disasters in far places.

Puggarees

Id, June 1953

Puggarees of fragile organdie seem to be the fashionable man's wear this Id. I have seen so many, all so pretty — and here are three for you ...

The old ruffian of a horse-dealer came with his small grand-daughter this morning to make Id greetings. He was dressed in his best; turquoise studs in his striped shirt; his smiling but battered visage topped with a dainty confection of pale yellow organdie, the long end left dangling over his shoulder in studied abandon to outline his left ear and golden ear-ring.

Another I saw was a 'bullocky' (Bylee-wallah in Urdu) who sang as he drove his white oxen to the stone quarries. His puggaree was zinnia red and spangled with little silver bits. It was the only concession to the festivities — or perhaps he had no change from the work-a-day soil-stained shirt and shalwar.

And now this evening the chokidar has arrived in the usual spotless white trousers topped with what can only be described as a dinner jacket of impeccable cut, no doubt inherited from his former employer. Gracing his handsome head is a puggaree, Rajput style, of the most delicious pale rose-pink organdie, putting one in mind of a débutante's dream frock. Meanwhile, the women all veil themselves with burkhas, poor peahens!

Motoring in Sind.

The new baby

June 7th

Early this morning, Kullander's wife gave birth to a boy — a tiny atom of pale brown flesh and a lot of black hair that came down over his cheeks like side-whiskers. A Dai, the native midwife, had attended and, even to my untrained eyes, the results didn't look too good. G. took me post-haste up to the little Mission where I made the acquaintance of M.M. who seemed to be surrounded by barking dogs and a bevy of pretty nurses in Pakistani dress. She got her things together at once, called Agnes, one of the pretty girls, and back we came.

While M.M. examined the little wife and babe, I fetched her basins and hot water and towels and cotton wool and the baby was made neat and tidy and bandaged over his tiny tum and the utterly filthy old Dai made to watch and given what was no doubt her very first lesson in midwifery. But though the two rooms and court-yard where Kullander lives are probably the most palatial he has ever had for his family (there are good servants' quarters here with

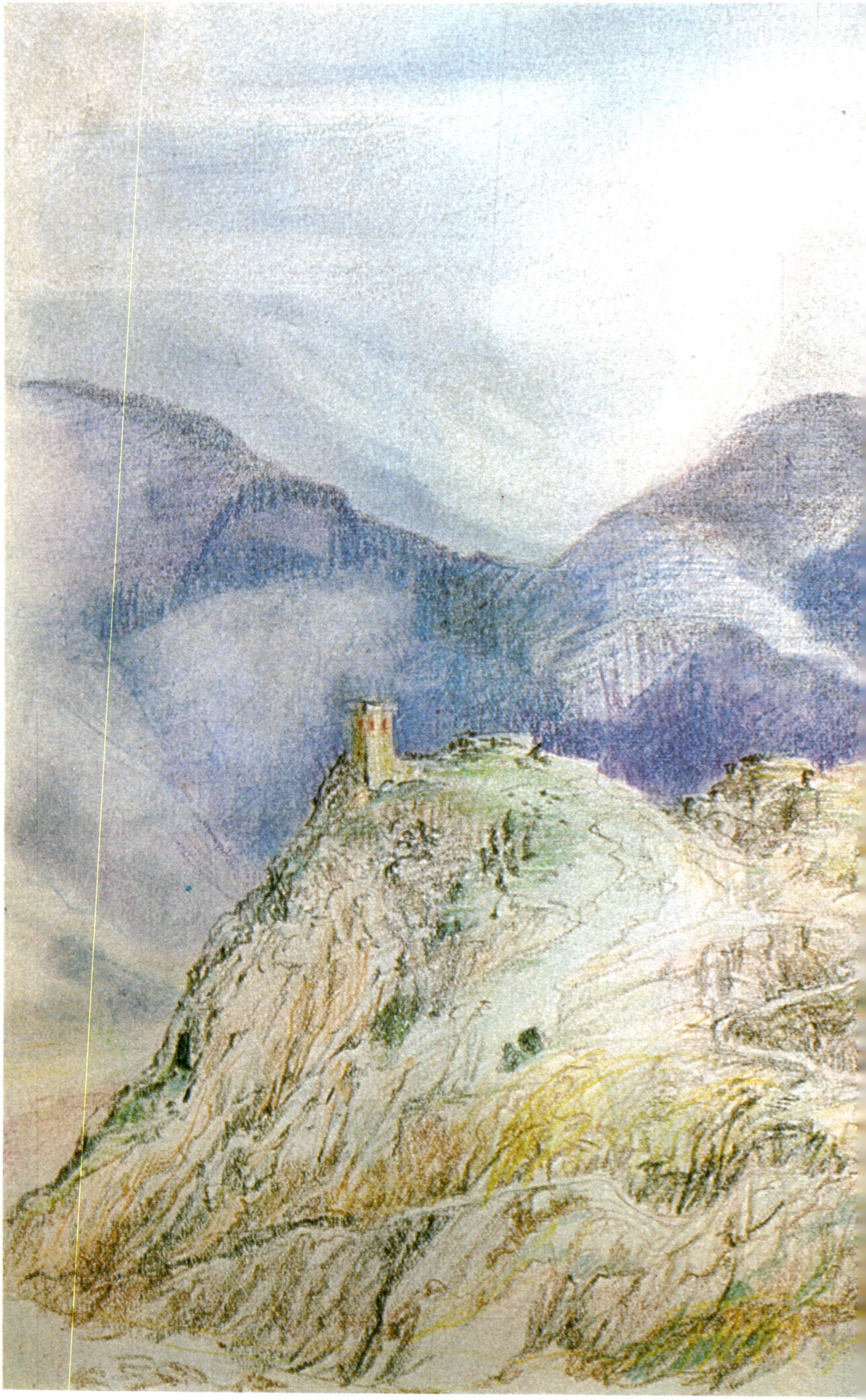

Mountain scene on the North-West Frontier.

electric light and a little bathing place) M.M. felt that the mother and babe would be better in a hospital bed where she could keep an eye on them. We quickly made the back of the station-wagon into an ambulance: put a mattress, rugs and quilt on the floor to make it soft, and then little M.M. picked up the mother and carried her over. There was a small fuss about 'purdah' and the woman had to have her face completely veiled in case some man saw her; then there was another small fuss because Taj Mohammed, aged four, insisted upon coming too — and then Kullander thought he had every right to travel with his family; and so they all squatted in the back of the car, M.M. supporting the mother's head and baby. And off we went.

In this country, all available relatives go to the Hospital to keep the patient company, get her food, provide conversation and make everything as homey as possible. In the higher-paying private rooms there are always at least two beds, one for the patient and one for the husband or perhaps the mother-in-law. The aunts, cousins, grandmothers and in-laws sit on the floor all day making hell's own din and chatter, only breaking off to spit pan — a leaf smeared with betel paste that they chew: if they are very refined, they will go outside the room and spit on the veranda — *if* they can be bothered to move!

Later

I took tins of the choicest delicacies from my store cupboard and sent them up to the Mission for the little wife — but have later discovered that Kullander took them all off to the bazaar, sold them and is making a whoopee evening on the proceeds, while the wife has had dry chapattis for supper — I suppose I was foolish to imagine the nice things would be given to her!

The old Dirzee

The old, old man, who sits on the veranda in front of one of the most ancient sewing machines anyone could possibly imagine, has the most amusing turns of speech concerning his work and always uses the American expressions, such as basting and bias, rather than tacking and on-the-cross, and some of his sentences can only have originated in a G.I. camp. G. to, whom I told this, says he was probably in the American Civil War! — and that remark has given me the first laugh today, which began as a morning of sadness.

Old dirzee.

Everest

You may be surprised to know that, according to the newspapers of Pakistan and Bharat, it was Tensing the Sherpa porter who was the *real* victor of Everest; and the British Expedition with its equipment to make the ascent possible, Colonel Hunt, Hillary and the other men are scarcely in the picture. Bharat has claimed Tensing as a Bharatti and says he planted *their* flag on the tip of Everest — in fact, a very phoney picture was shewn of this flag and pole at least six feet tall with him beside it and snowy wastes all around! I believe he has since denied this flag business but as the story has been printed in the paper, no doubt half the people in the world believe it implicitly. Here is a lovely bit of reportage for you:

> APHRODISIAC-MINDED INDIANS ... HINDUS
> 'And did the great height give you sexual stimulation?' to which Hillary replied that he hadn't given much thought to the matter.

Sukee

June 1953

Sukee, my small scrap of tabby kitten, is fascinated by the donkey we have in the garden; she creeps over the grass getting nearer and nearer until she is about half an inch away from his heels, her eyes glazed with admiration of such a huge beast. Up to now, the two Pariah dogs who have adopted us have been her idols and sometimes she is perilously near being gulped down with their dinner, so near does she creep to them; but today they are ignored and this sick and lame donkey which were are feeding and caring for until it is well enough to carry loads of stone again is her focal point.

The racing camel

June, 1953

Last night, the quick crash of bells brought me, inquisitive as a cat, to the veranda. The sounds I knew, and yet I couldn't place them until I

Camels being washed in Karachi.

saw in the semi-darkness the vague outline of a riding camel; and then remembered that the rapid movement, the tones of the bells, more familiar in the slow rhythm of pack camels, had, of course, altered.

A tall shape halted with a clash like cymbals and against the glare of the Petromax pressure lamp in the little wooden tea-shop opposite, I saw two figures upon a huge beast, silhouetted against the light.

With front knees down, then an undulating heave and subsidence as the back legs were folded, the camel knelt to let the figures jump off, then walk to chairs and drink tea in the evening hour. Their gossiping must have been of the camel, and one proudly wished to show her paces, and so, in a few minutes, mounted. There was another sprinkle of sound and the prehistoric form plunged past with incredible speed, the bells at her neck in harsh cacophony as they broke on the starlit night. Down the road to the sand-bluffs they sped, and after a fraction's silence came the swift start back. Then a spilling of laughter upon the darkness and applause to greet the return. Those brief moments made magic for me.

Karachi

We have been here in Karachi since Wednesday — meant to have gone back to Hyderabad yesterday, but G. is having a great deal of trouble getting new tyres for the car. It was new last Christmas, a big Chevrolet station-wagon, and was fitted with American tyres, which have completely worn out and *burst*. We had a dreadful journey down here with two punctures and a burst tyre, all very dangerous, and had to slow down to 25 m.p.h. all the time, taking from 7.30 a.m. till 4.30 p.m. to get here instead of doing it in 3¾ hours as usual.

The Pakistan government has stopped all imports of 'foreign' tyres and, as no such things are made in this country, lots of vehicles are just having to go off the road, buses and lorries as well as private cars and the few remaining tyres have jumped high in prices and most of them are on the Black Market (where practically everything else is) and are being held there. If you could only see the vast

Bride and silver jewellery.

queues of men who crowd the permit offices every day, their business at a standstill without tyres for their vehicles … it is pathetic. We just can't think what this country is doing to itself, but it seems like suicide. So many English and Continental firms have or are on the point of packing up and quitting the country, everything is coming to a standstill and these Pakistanis don't seem to have a clue how to run things and they certainly can't get on without imports. It is now the rarest thing to find a humble packet of Lux — it's not made here and not imported — there is a complete racket on any kind of soap. Fortunately I have a stock that should last me nearly a year. Cream for one's face and hands, so very necessary in the dry desert, is practically unprocurable. G. uses it as much as I do. Now that Nehru is trying to snatch Kashmir the Pakistanis are talking of war and arming etc., but I don't think they'll have a hope; no arms or munition factories were left in Pakistan, and all the huge wartime factories, which incidentally G. was in charge of, were all put to Nehru's side of the country.

The most terrific weather in Hyderabad has now passed and we feel almost cool with a temp. of 99 in the shade, and I can stay pottering in the garden (with my sunshade) until about 10 a.m. tho' after that it becomes a bit too warm for comfort. We had some simply amazing thunderstorms which started with a glowering violet sky, the great clouds coming slowly nearer until one felt suffocated, and then a thin wind would make a sudden sweep, blowing up the dust in spirals. And then, a complete tornado would whip down, taking away roofs, bowing the poor saplings to the ground and stopping all animal traffic. After a while RAIN — rain in quite unbelievable quantities simply deluged from the coppery purple clouds, so that all the roads were under water for hours afterards, and when the lights came on at night everything was reflected, making canals and lakes of what one knew to be really parade grounds and streets and gardens and giving everything a fantastic and Venetian quality — which was all right for us in a good high station-wagon, but for the people who live in reed matting or mud huts it was very terrible. Many were drowned and the old and very young have died from pneumonia.

    This kind of weather has been happening on and off for over a month and with so much water the long miles of desert that we pass through between Hyderabad and Karachi are now seas of *green* — not grass so much as a little juicy-leaved plant about six inches across which springs up at small intervals, and in the distance gives the illusion of a solid green mass. Soon, we shall have lived through a whole year of this desert life. Already we know that, for most of the year, the dry sand nullahs and wadis, some half a mile across, become during August roaring torrents of water that sweep away roads and livestock and even a huge 5-ton lorry in which two young men were drowned, as the whole vehicle was hurled onto its side and then submerged. It is all very interesting, as long as I am *not* expected to live here this time next year.

Village camels

The village camels which normally walk in a small circle, blindfold and harnessed to a Persian Wheel (which irrigates the small squares of fields as the pots and tins tied to the creaking wheel spill the precious water into a runnel which is connected to a ditch) are now wandering free, and browsing on the thorny caper bushes and barbul-trees. All the scorching summer they go around and around, doing eight-hour shifts in the blazing heat and the sun — and so, I suppose, they have done since Moses was a boy, tho' perhaps not the same camels! We have been to the Coronation film of 'A Queen is crowned' and it was such a wonder and glory that we went almost every night for week, hating to part with any fraction of the film, and we took all the servants, even the old Dirzee of 96 who happened to be sitting on the veranda doing a few days' work for us. They all loved to see their own Pakistan troops marching — and the English countryside as well as the gorgeous Abbey ceremony. *How* homesick I felt, quite desperately so!

August

Having dusted the sand from the typewriter with my handkerchief, I am ready to start a morning of letter-writing.

It is a lovely morning — a wind comes in through the half-open lattice of the veranda where I am sitting and in the small piece of cultivation outside I can see zinnias and big yellow sunflowers and pinky-orange cannas, as well as a patch of green grass and some quite healthy-looking hedge. None of these things were here when we came last Christmas — nor was the veranda trellis quite covered with a curtain of green creeper, as it is now. On some mornings, the thickly piled leaves are studded with mauve and white, like an English convolvulus; and the whole length of the trellised veranda which used to let in the scorching sun and desert dust is now perfectly insulated against the worst of the weather. If only the previous occupants had been garden-minded, the creepers might have been thick during the terrible heats of May and June. Ah well — the next occupants will benefit and not have to cope with desert up to the front door when they arrive!

Fishing with herons.

The happy household

Our happy household is *not* so happy and tall Sekander Khan has lost all patience with little Akbar the Hamal. The latter is so willing and yet so scatterbrained that he does the silliest things. For months now, he has every morning let down the bamboo chicks (rather like Venetian blinds) over the veranda trellis, so that the sun may be kept a little at bay during the great heat. But this morning, an hour after this ceremony, he has gone out to the oven-like veranda and rolled all the chicks up to the ceiling — says he forgot! So with things like this happening, Sekander announces that his patience is at an end. Akbar looks miserable and, being nervous, makes even more mistakes than usual. G. says that as Sekander is so grumpy we had better have a fresh lot of servants. I temporise by suggesting that as Sekander is very hard to please he had better choose a boy to suit himself — poor Akbar being the fourth we have supplied to the great man. So today Sekander has gone off to the Capital by train and I hope he will return in a better mood, accompanied by the Strong Boy of his dreams — which is not hopeful in this desert where nobody wishes to live and only exorbitant salaries will bring them.

Our pets and others

As I write, I can see Shamus the Tough Tom-cat over on the window-sill. He is stretched out on his back, his paws in the air and he has eaten too much breakfast; he is quite the greediest animal I have ever kept. His distended tummy is snowy white and his back tabby; how he manages to bend to wash himself I can't imagine. I call him my White Rabbit because he looks so pure and clean.

Toffee, the gay little girl with orange, black and lots of white colouring, is expecting kittens and nobody knows how; she is 'too young' we thought.

Blanche, the white lady shaped like a greyhound with lovely soft brown eyes and a tail she wags in circles like a clockwork toy, is, since her quite disgraceful behaviour with 'George Sanders' (there is *no* other name for him — a half bull-terrier, very pushful and thrusting) expecting puppies, and I don't know which will have her children first.

Besides these, we also feed two other dogs; and have Sukee, Little Black and the Joey, who are cats.

Lately, we have had a green parrot as a visitor, but we didn't keep her long. The old Padre has her in a cage and, when he told us that according to his certain knowledge she had not been out of it for twenty-five years, we invited her to come here for a holiday and live in a small separate veranda where she could stretch her wings. But alas — after so many years, she had lost the use of her muscles and all that she could do was to walk about on her heels in a puzzled way and then go and sit on the outside of her wire prison. She stayed there for hours on end, quite immobile, and so we came to the conclusion that she *liked* her cage and the old Padre. At first he told us that he was only too thankful to be rid of her, but now he tells us he had no idea he would miss a bird so much, and so we have taken her back and they are united — and I hope they are both happy.

Joey and the chiel

Joey was the tiniest kitten you ever saw. He wore a black fur coat, had bright beady eyes that really couldn't see properly and the *loudest voice.* Somebody had left him on a rubbish heap in the dirty crowded city.

When the kind Geoffrey passing in a car heard his frightened and hungry screaming, he picked him up and brought him home; and it was very difficult to know how to feed him because he

Young eagles.

hadn't learned to eat or lap milk out of a saucer. At first I tried to feed him with a silver spoon, but he just got his poor little black nose into the milk and blew bubbles and cried all the more. Then I tried condensed milk on the tip of a finger — this was better — he could suck the finger but he didn't like the sticky condensed milk and it upset his baby tummy. *Then* came the idea, and a little warm milk and fish was held in my hand which I curled up, and Joey buried his tiny face in the soft flesh and drank and sucked happily, because it felt like mother's soft tummy, which he used to snuggle against so long ago.

Now, in this house also lived four other cats — there was Shamus, the old Tom, rather fat and rather bad-tempered and 'Bosscocky' of them all, whose favourite position was asleep upside down on a window-sill; as you know, I called him my White Rabbit. Then there was Sukee, who had the softest fur and sleepy eyes; she didn't mix much with the other cats, whom she thought rather vulgar, and between themselves they nicknamed her the Princess. Next came Toffee, a jolly little red-haired minx, who used to tweak Sukee's tail, wait for her around corners and jump out on her and who didn't care a bit for Sukee's fine manners.

And last came Little Black, a very young boy who had a great reverence for the others. But Old Tom Shamus ignored the youngster, which made him feel shy. Sukee, who rather liked all the notice, was upset if she saw anyone new; Toffee was too gay and too busy chasing little frogs and butterflies, which she never caught, to take any notice of him, and so he had rather a lonely life, especially when he felt it safer to hide from the others. Sukee had once been so rude and unkind to him that he hurt his leg in trying to jump onto a shelf which was too high for him, and so was put in a lovely basket all by himself on a cushion, and the others kept away from him.

On the day when they all first saw Joey they were *quite horrified* (as all big cats are of tiny kittens, if you have noticed). Shamus stepped back, said 'Kharr-Ffouff' and then darted off and drank up everybody's breakfast milk as fast as his tongue would lap. Sukee said 'Hiss-ttt' and walked away, also rather quickly, because she had never had any kittens. Toffee at first thought he was a new kind of insect and tried patting him to see if he would jump. This frightened him and he gave the tiniest 'Spattt!' at her — and so she ran off too. Little Black, who was sitting on the edge of the circle because he was still much in awe of them all, stretched out his neck and took a sniff at Joey, who was still all of a bristle. Joey smelt 'black', which was a comfort to a lonely black kitten, and Little Black smelt 'black' to Joey who was longing for his black mother. Then Little Black licked Joey's face once or twice, which knocked him down as his legs were not yet used to obeying him; and I was glad they were going to be friends and put Joey into the lovely basket on a bit of Little Black's cushion and left them together.

Now, after a little while, when Little Black's leg was getting better and Joey could wobble-walk fairly well, I took them out to the garden and put them on the grass together. This was the first grass that Joey had ever felt; it was springy and awfully long and he just didn't know what to do with his feet. Little Black sat up and ate a blade or two in a superior way — he had heard it was good for the digestion. But when he saw Toffee stalking a dragonfly, he left off and made himself small, because he was still really very timid and afraid of everybody except Joey and me.

At the end of the garden there was a tree, and, very high up, two chiels had a large untidy nest full of young and always hungry babies. The chiels had to keep flying all the day to find enough food to put into the ever-open mouths of their children — here a piece of bread, there a small meaty bone — sometimes a mouse or little bird — all was taken straight to the hungry babies. *So,* the day they saw tiny Joey on the lawn they had an idea. *But,* whenever they wheeled overhead, sliding down the wind with outstretched wings, I was always standing by Joey and lame Little Black and they just had to slide off again and try somewhere else.

Then, one morning, the old gardener wanted to show me some new plants he had brought, and for a few moments I forgot to keep an eye on the chiels. With a swoosh and whirl of beating wings, the chiel swooped down on Joey and was up again without touching the ground — but another chiel who happened to be passing had seen Mother Chiel with a tasty morsel and, also being hungry, dived into her to take it from her. And so they clashed and in the argument dropped little Joey, who was screaming blue murder, with a plonk. Little Black, quite quite terrified with all the noise of wings and general commotion, sat frozen with fright — but then, when Joey landed with the plonk, he realised that something was amiss with his little friend and rushed up to him as fast as his poor hurt leg would let him and *stood over* him, *just* in time to save him from the Mother Chiel who by this time had seen off the stranger and was again diving down to clutch poor Joey in her feet. But *no!* There stood Little Black and he forgot his fright and that he was a timid little lame cat and he spat and he hissed and the fur bristled on his back and tail — and with all the noise the white dog Blanche came rushing out and I came rushing back and Toffee rushed across the grass like a yellow streak of light after her dragonfly and Shamus and Sukee emerged from nowhere — and there was a *tremendous* fuss! Poor Joey was quite dazed, but not very much hurt and later, when he had got over his wounds, he used to tell his story to the others and boast how wonderful it was to be able to fly! But Little Black was the hero of the hour. Old Tom Shamus said 'Jolly well done, for a youngster — you might like to come with me on my next mouse hunt' and Little Black *glowed* with pride.

Sukee bowed to him, murmured 'How brave you are'; Toffee brought him a dead moth she had found and said 'Let's be friends' and Old Tom Shamus, before he stretched himself out upside down on the window-sill, yawned his approval.

And so, thanks to Joey and the chiel, everyone was friendly and happy. But Joey didn't go out into the garden for a long time after that: playing among the flower-pots was safer!

A dinner party

Hyderabad, Sind; August, 1953

Dinner party.

Tonight we have a dinner party. The old Padre, the little Irish nurse who runs the midwife training school, the delightfully mad foreign doctor and a wonderful old Missionary-lady who is of enormous heart as well as girth. We send the Station-Wagon with Syed Mohammed very smart in khaki uniform and peaked Driver's hat worn at an angle over his Pathan bobbed hair, to do a round tour of collection, and we first sit under the Chinese lanterns hanging by the veranda and chatter over the before-dinner drinks. Sekander Khan knows every guest's favourite tipple. Chilled tomato juice for Mission, milk and ginger beer for the Church, lemon squash and soda for the Maternity Home and rum and lime for the lady doctor. The cats come and join the party, Little Black taking great fancy to the Padre, Toffee who can't resist the Doctor, who can well resist her, as she can't bear any animal to touch her, and Shamus, who talks in long drawly wails, telling all who may understand what a terrible time he had last night out behind the servants' quarters with the other toms of the neighbourhood. We who smoke say we are keeping off the mosquitoes and midges; after a while the tall white figure of Sekander Khan stands framed in the creeper-covered doorway and announces dinner; which, after the Padre's grace, usually becomes a very serious half-hour of concentrated eating, punctuated by the Doctor's demands for a cigarette between courses and apologies for her bad manners in wanting one. Then coffee in the sitting-room, the largest and heaviest bodies being guided to the strongest of our collection of dicky chairs; and G. and I just sit back and let the chat of Mission 'shop' flow backwards and forwards.

The rains

30th August, 1953

Do you care for thunderstorms? I always feel on the tip-toe of excitement! We have had some rather amazing ones lately, starting with a glowering violet sky and great clouds coming slowly nearer until one felt suffocated; then a thin wind would make a sudden sweep, blowing up the dust in spirals, and finally a complete tornado would whip down taking way tin roofs, bowing the poor saplings to the ground and stopping all animal traffic. After a while rain — rain in quite unbelievable quantities, simply deluged from coppery purple clouds, so that all the roads were under water for hours afterwards. At night, when the lights came on, everything was reflected, making canals and lakes of what one knew to be parade grounds and streets and gardens, and giving the dull desert a fantastic Venetian quality. This kind of weather has been happening on and off for over a month and, with so much water, the long miles of desert are now seas of green.

Blanche's babies

Back last night from the Capital, to find (a) your lovely long letter (b) the Mali hadn't been bothering to water, and if we had come one day later the garden, such as it is, would have withered up (c) Blanche had had *ten* puppies.

Blanche — I must tell you about poor Blanche. I had judged that her puppies were due in about ten days' time, and when we simply had to go to the Capital for a few days I told Sekander Khan to look after her and feed her well and see that she had her special rug in a cool spot on the veranda. Perhaps she was upset not to see me; anyway, she ran off into the desert and Sekander sent G. a telegram (which was not shown to me in case I fretted, which I should have done) to say that she was missing. Then he went out to search for her and found her in some jungle with *ten* shrieking pups and she so weak and done for that he had to carry her back in his arms, while the two other men brought the puppies and they were all put on her rug here. That was rather good for Muslims, don't you think? Usually, they will never let a bitch come near to them, saying it is unclean.

The number of small wriggling bodies was quite fantastic — they seemed to take turns in relays for the 'tea-cups' while Blanche lay with a baffled look in her lovely hazel eyes, quite unable to connect all the fun-and-games she indulged in two months ago with this Nemesis. But after dinner we took away six little girls and put them in a big box with a cotton wool and a whiff of chloroform and all was over painlessly.

Blanche and puppy.

The twangy-wangy man

Because feather pillows are a rarity and also *hot,* we have cotton filling, but it soon goes into lumps and then the cotton man has to be summoned to fluff them up again. As nobody knows exactly where he lives, he must be caught on the wing, so to speak, as he goes past our compound. He walks along pulling the wire string of his strange machine so that it twangs a small tune and thus advertises himself. Sekander Khan ushered him onto the veranda a few days ago, and the bolster, cushions and pillows were decanted in front of him. He commenced by hanging his bow with its long string high on the wall. From this is supended the strong harp-like contrivance for teasing wool and in his hand he held a black pointed dumb-bell for banging the single string. Whang! whang! whang! and he grunted in unison with each stroke. The cotton is caught and flung upwards in small clouds; the finest flutters like thistledown in the air, and the rest piles up in a soft mass against the wall. But with all these airy mountains of fluff and cotton dust I begin to wonder if it is worth it. Half the bungalow seems filled with throat-catching flurries of fine cotton, which I am certain will linger for weeks.

Later, he refills all the empty covers, beating them into shape with a round stick. Finally he takes a dirty little bag, a needle and thread and sews up the seams most beautifully; once again we can sleep on soft pillows!

The twangy-wangy man.

Goat taxi

We start today by being taxi to a couple of goats — in this manner:

Past the bungalow all day long go herds of cattle, sheep and goats, and the tinkle-tonk tinkle-tonk of the bells at their necks is mingled with their bleating and the shrill cries of the urchins in charge. The goats are big and long-coated, with ears a foot long in the Sindi fashion; some are as high as calves and have a wicked look in their white eyes as they trot on tiny feet and flick their upturned tails.

On the other side of the road is a small shack — 'hotel' in this country — where the passers-by may enjoy a glass of char and a chapatti for a small sum, and here the goatherds sometimes stop.

But the two black nannies I saw yesterday were being carried and at the tea-shop were laid on the ground; later, when the herdsman tried to make them stand, they swayed and wobbled on their poor stiff legs. Together we went across to enquire the trouble and found the wretched animals all but lifeless, their aged bones making shelves for the dull black skin and hair that held their frames together. We called over for a bucket of water, which they sipped, closing their tired eyes the while. The herdsman volunteered that they were going to market for slaughter and that as he was paid R.1 a month each for their care, the two sickly old ladies must arrive live to be counted. The usual crowd had collected and there was a great deal of chat between a tonga-load of men, a Police guard and all the tea-shop customers and, while the babel continued, we decided that we would bring up the Station-Wagon for the old nannies and take them up the long hill to the market to save them the torture of walking. The herdsman was thrilled at the thought of a ride and, leaving the rest of his charges to be walked in by his small son, clambered in the back amongst the goats and Arloo, who had joined the crowd again after taking the bucket back.

Down the tightly-packed streets of the old bazaar, past ancient houses and the even more ancient smells of the overcrowded East, we were directed by the herdsman, with toothless Arloo as chorus. When we saw a stall selling green lucerne we bought some and the starved animals were fed with small handfuls. Finally, we reached what can only be named the Street of Goats. Hundreds of them were being herded into small mud-walled compounds covered with a latticed roof of thorn, and an old old man with a long white beard skilfully counted them as they rushed and bucked forward through the narrow doorway to the bleating throng within. We left our old ladies with their bunch of lucerne by the wall to await the rest of the herd and then walked back to the car.

Cries for help

To Lt. Col. G. Swayne thomas Sahib Bahader and madum

Sir,
Respectfully i have Receeved A letter from my family thy want on hundred Rupees Rs 100 so i have not got ther for i want going to Karachi there are Living my friend i will ask him for som Rupees if hi can give me then i will send to my family. Pleas i want to meet with my frind Padre in Karachi also — so if you can help me of Rs 100 one hundred Because i can not got mony from any Body else i hop you will help me sire and you can cut down my PAy.
Sir i am your must obediently servant
$\qquad$ Sikander Khan.

Telegramme from Roomi...

Your telegrams informed accordingly if neede shall be at your service in mimimized duration. Roomi....
(Coming quickly ?)

1.9.53 PeTITION from Said Mohammed

Pleas sir
i need Rupees 20 twenty Because my father going to Home on the 10.9.53.
i want to help them Rs60.0.0.
i hap sir you will help me on this time
thanks Very much sir
i am your most obediently servant   SaidMahd.

OVER
Received Rupees twentyonly Advance on date 1/9/53
gludly with thanks too much...
$\qquad$ SaidMahd.

Envelope addressed to G. from Hassan Mahd Khan, Oct, 4th, 1953.

   Luentinent Cornal
   Swani Thomas Town planning
   Suppendandent Engineer
   Sind HaidaraBad
   Baraj Kalooni Banglow No.I.

The hiss

Hyderabad, October, 1953

Goodness *how* this house stinks of ONIONS — and all because the Consamer (cook) says that SNAKES hate the smell.

I must tell you of an adventure we had last night. From a wonderful deep sleep I was awakened by a noise which was exactly like a steam train in Euston Station, and really very loud indeed — loud even above the two electric fans, which are by no means silent, but one gets used to their whirr. Fortunately, I put on my side-lamp before getting out of bed to look. Blanche was lying on the rug asleep, but little Toffee, the kitten, was skittering around very much awake and teasing a great coil of BROWN SNAKE, which was partly under a chair, its head ready to strike. I leaned over to G's bed and woke him; he said sleepily 'Where — where? I can't see any snake' and then *did* and nearly passed out! He is really frightened of snakes which I am not, though I have a deep respect for them. On the other hand, had the snake been a spider, I should have fainted on the spot. I tried to put my flimsy dressing-gown over my still more flimsy nightgown, picked up Toffee, he pushed out Blanche all in the twinkling of my eye, and after having the presence of mind to shut the two bedroom doors after us, we stood out on the veranda wondering what to do next. We could hear the steam engine still keeping up its loud noise, and as we peered through the fly-screen window, we could just see it, still darting out its long tongue but otherwise immobile.

After a few minutes, we 'came to' and called the Chokidar. Then we called Sekander Khan who sleeps in the house; he came armed with a chunk of wood shaped like a hockey stick. Then I gave them my furlined Brevitts and my desert ankle boots, and G., who was now dressed, put on his desert boots, and the three of them went in to deal with the Hissing Viper, while Toffee and I stood on the veranda and looked through the fly wire.

The important thing was to hit it first, otherwise it might get away under the wardrobe or chest of drawers; as it was half under a chair, a direct whack was not easy. But the Chokidar gave it one great blow with his dundee and broke its back; Sekander, not to be outdone, bashed its head with his hockey stick and G. followed suit with a curtain pole, so that it was very dead in a short time. When the Chokidar held it at arm's length by its tail, it measured over four feet and left a trail of blood over the tiled floors. I am certain that if Toffee hadn't teased it and made it hiss, one of us would probably have stepped on it and been bitten — which is well-nigh fatal of course. So this morning the Cook has come in with pounds and pounds of ONIONS, and all the water outlets in the bathroom where anything can creep in (and little frogs do) have been rubbed with raw onions till our eyes cry. He assures us that snakes hate the smell of onions — I certainly do!

The Chokidars

All through the night the Chokidars call to each other 'Kabardaaaar! Kabardaaaar!' (which means 'Beware!'). Sometimes four voices at different distances have games of calling and answering, to break the monotony of the darkness — perhaps to let the thieves know their whereabouts! Their voices are echoing and powerful and I have a theory that Chokidars are chosen for their vocal chords and not their brawn.

The caravan

A great caravan has just passed. Long before it came into view, I could hear the bells 'like an awful lot of ice in a wooden jug' as G. says; and as the soft-footed beasts went rhythmically past, they were silhouetted against the bright acetylene lamp of the little tea-shop.
      Before the light faded, great herds of sheep and goats were being driven down the road, the boys in charge being almost invisible through the clouds of soft dust that surrounded the animals like a halo. The countless little goat feet made a sound like the rustle of dried leaves.

Mianee

Did I tell you that we went to re-visit Mianee — or Mirrani as the Sindi milestones call it — last Sunday? No — I think not, as my diary says I last posted a letter to you on Saturday. The Memorial took quite a lot of finding as the jungle and the barbul-trees now grow quite up to it. In 1940 we went out there on camels — there was desert all round and the obelisk was visible a long way off. Then we went across country (last Sunday I mean) to Mattiari, the rather fascinating and jumbled native town halfway to Hala, and looked at a most beautifully painted Tomb. All the inside walls were of white shell plaster and every bit coloured and decorated in the Persian manner — all done about 100 years ago by some of the Persian community which lived in Mattiari — with two saints who reclined under green and red silks and marble tombs dated from 12th century. I have never seen such a lovely and colourful mausoleum — here and there in the free-running patterns of flowers and stems were pieces of mirror, adding to the richness of the designs, and the dome was fully ornamented with mirror and gold and rich medallions. Hanging were three glass and silver lamps and I thought it must have looked exquisite at night with the soft glow reflected on the walls a thousand times. A young English-speaking man who insisted upon being our honorary guide, said 'yes' *but* soon Mattiari was going to have electricity in the town and *then* — the walls would have nice bright electric lights and NEON STRIPS.

Today, after lunch, we are going out to the Forest Bungalow at Hatri which is only seven miles from here, and we shall stay the night and come back here for breakfast.

Just a short weekend

We have been to Hatri, staying in the little Forest Bungalow, which was once the shooting lodge of a Mir. It is built twenty feet high on a brick and plaster platform and the trees that surround it bow over the whitewashed edges of the low wall of the terrace, casting deep shadows on the sun-lit paving. I wanted to sleep on the roof amongst the great trees there and hear the Dawn Chorus in the early cool of the desert, there are such lovely birds out there.

Up among the branches green parrots nest and quarrel and make love and shriek joyously from dawn to sunset; they descend in emerald flights from the gentian skies, their long tails spread fanwise as they alight in a glint of green feathers and red beaks. Grey-headed crows dispute possession of the great banyan-trees and yellow-beaked minas mimic the noisy battle derisively. There is a walled stairway of about twenty steps leading from the garden to this terrace and, as soon as the dusk falls, all the frogs in creation take it into their heads to hop up the steps. I can't imagine why they should want to leave the garden with its running stream of nice dark brown water and lush grass — perhaps there are little insects to entice them, I certainly had my bare legs bitten as we sat aloft over our drinks, watching the thin new moon rise between the night-dark branches. The Bearer brought out a tall iron rod, bent like a shepherd's crook and fixed to a heavy base, and hung on it a storm-lantern; but it was a pale light compared to the luminous whiteness of the fireflies that danced amongst the shadowy trees. Small bats flitted edgewise around us and everything was perfectly quiet for a long time; so lovely and remote.

And now let me tell you what we have to take with us for

The Temple, Hala.

a night in the country. First, our pillows, sheets, mosquito nets, towels and bathmat, all laid out in the proofed canvas bed-roll which in this country is called a bistra. Then our washing things, soap and toothmugs and face-cloths are all put into the enamel wash-basin, which has a fitted leather top to fasten under the bowl's rim. Then comes the packing of shoes and a change of clothes and our night attire; also the electric torch and the small Browning pistol 'just in case'.

In the kitchen, the cook, perspiring and apprehensive, is fitting up the tiffin-carrier. This is an invaluable affair which is composed of four aluminium flat-sided bowls which fit on top of one another and are held together by a long handle which slides through slots, the base of each bowl acting as a lid for the next till the top, which has a tightly fitting lid. In this is put our cooked lunch; rice at the bottom, next the curried eggs, then some tomatoes and, in the top, wheaten chapattis — very compact.

Then in another box are the cooking-pots and frying-pan

and kettle; and all the other things that always make such a clatter. Then the Thermos flasks, two with cold boiled water and one with ice in chunks; tea-towels and soap and the dish-mop too, and some vegetables to cook with the evening's omelette. Coffee and tea; milk in a bottle and butter in a crock all packed round with ice. Then the cat's dinner and breakfast (boiled fish — she is fussy). On the back veranda there is a smell of paraffin oil, as the gallon drum is found to have lost its bung and some of the oil has spilt. The two table lamps and three hurricane 'buttees', which are always packed in their cardboard boxes ready for the 'off', are now lined up by the Sweeper for my inspection. He stands holding his rush broom over his shoulder like a rifle. His bucket and cloths and bottle of Phenyle join the lamps in the back of the car.

Beggar at the mosque in Hatri.

The fat-tailed sheep

The other morning to the tea-shop across the road went a young man followed by his pet fat-tailed sheep. It was beautifully smooth and white and had little henna-dyed tufts of wool left uncut down the centre of its back, and wore a tinkly bell held by a necklace of turquoise blue beads to ward off the evil eye. About five Pi-dogs set up a shocking barking as the jolly little sheep with its enormous cushion of a tail went past, but it took absolutely no notice and followed its master into the shanty.
    Now this morning they have passed again and, as it is Sunday, G. is with me in the garden and we have hailed the bearded owner and asked him if his sheep would like to eat our grass while I do a quick sketch and G. takes a photograph. He is most obliging and they both come with hesitant steps to the lawn. Sukee rushes up from absolutely nowhere and does her usual inquisitive inspection. The sheep is not sure about cats and trots back to its master for protection, tossing its head and making the little bell ring merrily.

The Chokidar

This evening, as we were sitting having our drinks before dinner, the stately Chokidar, clad as usual in well-fitting dinner jacket and with a fresh organdie puggaree on his head, came over the grass and standing a little to one side, gave a most beautiful salute. After a small silence, I asked him if he had a petition (the signs were obvious!) and so he then took courage and asked G. if he might have four days' leave. His Mamoon (maternal aunt) was sick and he wished to visit her — his white whiskers gave the lie to a grandmother — but she was far away and the journey long. As this sudden solicitude for a female relative seemed exceptional, we hid our smiles and G. said he might go. With a deep salaam he departed around to the back of the house where the servants all sit and chat over a communal hookah during this evening hour — and I would like to bet his words to the fraternity were something like 'Well, boys, that one worked!'

Puppy and the Mali.

November morning

The mornings are now wonderful; the sun rises in misty splendour and I have discarded my fluffy dressing-gown and wear a dark blue velvet one for my 6 a.m. 'gardening'. The zinnias look as though Autumn were really here and have a 'touched by frost' air, which is, of course, sheer affectation; frost has never been known in Hyderabad, I am sure. The old Mali goes around gathering the yellowed leaves from shrubs and creepers, and the cats and puppy play in the pile; when he becomes furious and shoos them off, the puppy runs away with his pointed-toe Punjabi shoes or the large square of cotton that he wears over his turban, peasant fashion, to keep his ears warm in the early cold. It amuses me to see this womanly head-dress with a great tuft of grey beard poking out in front! But, later on, the days are still quite hot and though we have breakfast on the veranda, we have to retreat to the dining-room under a fan for luncheon.

A stray white donkey has just put his head through the veranda window. Goodness knows where he has come from — he must have heard we like animals! Today I saw a gaily decked horse: silver bridle, plume on his head and the finishing touch was a pair of small circular ear-rings, one through each nostril. In this country, camels wear bracelets of small jingling bells, so that there is music with each step.

The Padre's capes

Late November

I must tell you — it was so amusing. On the trip to the Missionary house at Tundo Alleyluia last week, we had the old Padre as one of our passengers, and it was a great day for him, as he never moves away from his tiny dust-covered bungalow. But that day was his birthday and he decided to celebrate. At heart, he is just a rather fussy old woman and always carries little bags and wraps and sling-purses around with him, and I constantly expect to see knitting-needles protruding. For the trip, he wore a twee little cloth cape he had designed himself and got the local Dirzee to make up for him; it had lots of patent fastenings and took ages to put on or take off, and I felt that in the still baking heat he must feel stifled, but he thought he might — just possibly — feel chilly in the car. Then, on the journey he confided to G. that in his little embroidered bag he had brought two more capes, also just in case. So later on, G. suggested that he changed to the mink, or perhaps would like his ermine for the journey back — great joke!

The evenings

In the evenings, as we sit outside in basket chairs, waiting for a cool breeze, the same things happen almost every night — some things are always the same.

1. Down the road and across the desert track leading to the walled British Cemetery, goes a hooded victoria. The horse keeps a slow even trot and hangs his head as though burdened with sadness, and in the carriage is a lady dressed in black with a long veil over her face. When the carriage reaches the Gothic stone gatehouse of the Cemetery the driver is left to smoke his Biri for the best part of an hour while the lady goes down the darkening path between the trees to the graves. I have never seen her unveiled, but been told that she is a Hindu, still quite young and comely and that since her dearly-beloved Christian husband died some years ago she has visited his grave every evening. And, as if to keep company with his hard last resting place, she has ever since slept lying on the floor and never on the bed that they shared. Perhaps this nightly pilgrimage to the Cemetery soothes the sorrow she must still feel.
2. From behind a flower-pot of ferns, which the Mali insists upon placing by the doorstep, a cricket starts his song, and Sukee hurls herself into the air after tiny white moths.
3. The garden lizard climbs up the tall zinnias and tries first one and then another stalk, before he finally settles himself upside down to sleep under a flower. His tiny hands grasp the ridged stem and his very long tail looks like a piece of loose string waving in the breeze.
4. Along the road come two brown bullocks slowly pulling a cart with creaking wheels and the driver is always wailing a thin reedy song.
5. From the darkness behind us, the evening bat slips past to the grey mist that was the sunset; and a few seconds later comes another, dipping like a swallow, and they fly together towards the dusty memory of the fading day.
6. From a small flower-bed comes a frog. Every evening he does this, and every evening at least one of the cats sees him and pats him; he then stays quite still for a while looking like a little grey stone, before starting again towards the mali-tank. As the tank is at least a hundred yards away, we can't think why he doesn't live by the water instead of making this precarious journey each time.
7. Down the road come the flip-flap flip-flap of loose sandals and two voices. The men themselves are invisible in the darkness.
8. Much later, when we have, as a rule, finished our dinner, we hear the S.P.R. bugler play the Last Post. He does it quite beautifully and we both fly back in memory to the Frontier days when G. was a Mountain Gunner up in Baluchistan where the nightly silver strains of the Last Post echoed around the great mountains to break the weird silence of the northern night.
9. Then still later, quite without fail, the jackals run in packs across the Ridge of the Tombs, screaming their demoniac defiance to the ghosts of departed Mirs, and all the Pariah dogs come out of their holes in the desert to make the night hideous with hysterical barking.

Village scene under a neem tree.

Old bottles

A Bottley-wallah goes through the compound; his distinctive cry, which at home would be 'any old rags-er-booones', starts with a thin high wail on the 'bottleyee' and comes down the scale with a sudden dash to the 'waaaaall-AH!' Usually Bottley-wallahs carry a sack for the collection of old bottles and tins that the Bearers sell them for a few annas, but this man appears to be the modern and sophisticated type and carries two SUITCASES!

November

It is the end of November and still warm enough to sit out under the stars and drink our evening rum. The Tombs of the Mirs and the little Mosque across the road are silhouetted against the deep blue of the glittering sky, and somewhere nearby a dog howls in primeval misery. Suddenly, there is a flare of fireworks and a distant drum beats out with throbbing rhythm, and I remember that when we passed through the small bazaar earlier this evening we saw men laying out mats and rugs before the door of a brightly-lit house, while a red-coated band stood around in a circle, the traffic just missing their coat-tails. Obviously a marriage, and everybody getting worked up for tomorrow, Friday, which is a most favoured day for weddings.

Late November

As I write, looking through the veranda window, I can see Akbar and the driver, Said Mohammed, leading in a donkey that G. has taken off the road. It has a terribly sore back and its poor bones stick out like knives. From nowhere in particular comes Sukee, making her way across the grass to inspect the new arrival. I have told you before that she adores other animals and particularly donkeys. The Mali is driving a stake into the ground for the long rope that the men lead her with, but I should not think there is the slightest chance that she will want to leave us. The heavy load is off her back and the grass is green. On the road, a coolie goes loping past with two great circular baskets suspended from a yoke on his shoulders. In the baskets are piled saffron-yellow, green and pink sweetmeats, which are lovely to look at but shocking to taste, I should think!

There was a mad dog around last night and now everyone is talking about the Chokidar who was bitten. We have sent him up to the hospital for injections of anti-rabies serum. His hand is covered in thick bandages, but his hawk-like face with long grey curls and beard is cheerful.

The Mistris

As I write, there is a Mistri (carpenter) hammering and sawing and mending our long wooden boxes — a sure sign that we shall soon be on the move again. These particular boxes are much travelled, having been made in Calcutta in 1946 to take home our superfluous junk. They went to England, then out to Australia and then back again here. They look rather like vast coffins but, when not travelling, they have elegant covers and are topped with tufted mattresses and make quite nice-looking banquettes. But after all these years, they are just a little broken and one needs a whole new top.

The first carpenter came last August; he had charming manners and made a little bow with his hands folded when he met us. Then he respectfully left his shoes on the doorstep and came in to

Craftsmen at work.

At the Tomb of the Mirs.

measure. All the clothes and oddments were taken out of the box and then he said he hadn't any tape or pencil or paper and so G. did the job for him. He left, promising that the new lid would be ready in a week. That was *grand,* we thought — at last we are far-seeing and having things done in good time! After three weeks, we called at his shop and again his delightful manners won our hearts in spite of the fact that he had not attempted to start the work. But, after another visit a few weeks later, we came to the conclusion that perhaps he never intended to start, and after a while G. found another carpenter to come to us.

He was entirely without any exterior polish or even cleanliness — in fact, so dirty that I didn't like to have him in the house. He also hadn't anything to measure by and so again we supplied all his wants and he departed saying he would come back in two days' time with the top cut. In about a week he returned, with pieces of wood so cracked and warped that they were only fit for firewood, and so once again all the clothes that had been hauled out of the boxes were put back and he was sent off.

At the beginning of this month, our little man Allahditta sent us yet another Mistri and again the same farce was gone through. All the contents of the box taken out, the boxes brought on to the veranda and measurements taken and a firm promise of immediate co-operation made. Yesterday morning, No. 3 turned up, minus wood, just to leave his tools and then vanished — perhaps to look for the Walrus — as the farce becomes more 'Alice' every time, and it is this week that I must start packing. But an hour ago, I saw his dirty-red tarbush nodding with the Mali's pink puggaree — and now his saw is wailing merrily!

A misty morning.

Ramadan

It is the month of Ramadan and everybody has been out looking for the new moon. Muslims all over keep fast for a lunar month and in this scorching weather it must entail great hardship and will-power. Not even a drop of water must pass their lips before sundown. Then, as the sun sinks and after a given signal, they will eat and drink — and again before the dawn, which heralds another day of fast. Only travellers and children and women with child are exempt from this strict custom. It really upsets me to have my fasting servants wait upon us at mealtimes and, in theory, I feel that I should join them in the fast.

At twilight, the Mosque lights up and we can see the devout Muslims, white-robed and hatted — some white-bearded too — standing at prayers; then they suddenly vanish from view below the window level as they fall to their knees, to rise after a few minutes and repeat the process. In a moment of naughtiness, I once called it playing 'bottoms up' and the phrase is apt! The Mullahs, or priests, make what can only to Western ears be called a HOWL — and this continues all through the evening. About 2.30 a.m. we are awakened by the most deafening clanging and bashing of tin trays and saucepans as the faithful are called to the last meal before sunrise. When this din drops, and the barking and howling Pi-dogs have settled down, we try to sleep, usually to be wakened again by over-zealous chokidars who call to each other all night — but whether to keep thieves or ghosts away or just for company, I don't know! I remember in the tea gardens of Nilgiris, they used to blow conch shells all night, but that was to frighten the panthers, they said.

The horse

A few days ago, quite early in the morning when we were all loaded up and starting for Karachi, I had a rather 'untoward' adventure with a big, yellow, crop-eared creature, the watch-dog of a tribe of nomads. As we passed along the Giddu road to Kotri bridge we saw, at a watering-trough, a crowd of beggary-looking people and a big man, who had a horse held in front of him while he belaboured its head with a stick as thick as my wrist. I stopped the car and G. and the driver and the Orderly all fell out and rushed to the man to stop this terrible beating of a defenceless animal — the man was holding its head near him on a very short rein and it just couldn't dodge the blows. When I had turned the engine off and put on the brakes, I followed. G. was then trying to take the horse from the man and hit him instead — the women were all shouting — the children yelling and crying — somewhere a dog was barking — but I didn't see where until I felt teeth in my bare leg and found this great, yellow dog, held on a chain by a boy just near to me. But I was so concerned for the horse which was the poorest, skinniest and most underfed beast I have *ever* seen — and that is saying a lot. It was blind in one eye, blood was on its forehead and around its eye; blood was coming from its mouth and the sides of its lips were raw; it had cuts which were still bleeding around its ankles and when, eventually, we made the man take off the saddle, with its high Sindi crupper, we found under the rags and bits of string, that the *whole length* of the poor animal's back was like raw meat.

As there was such a din going on, with the wailing of the

women and children and the shouting of the men, we went back into Hyderabad for the police, found one by the Circuit House and made him get into the car with me and only then did I realise that my leg was hurting and the car floor had my good red blood dripping over it — Goodness, *what* a morning! We got the policeman to walk the horse in and turned back to see the D.S.P. who was with the Collector so we went chasing him. Then I poured some Dettol onto my leg and *pushed back* the bits of me that were sticking out of the deep bite, tied some lint around and after a lot more palaver with the police to make sure the horse would be sent to the Veterinary Hosp. [now nearly defunct, but the only place to send animals] we then thought we had better check up on the dog in case it was rabid. So back towards Kotri and found the tribe with the dog, took it to the Giddu police and told them to keep it under observation until we returned from Karachi in a week's time. G. gave the young man who owned it five rupees for food for the dog, and I sent it four lovely chappatis, as it looked a very thin and hungry animal in spite of its largeness — and so, two and a half hours late, we proceeded on our way to Karachi. On our way we had two punctures and a burst tyre and the journey took seven hours instead of 3½! Hardly our day, one might say.

Now we are back. The poor horse will be destroyed as it is far too ill and weak even to really walk — *but* it has had ten days of *not* being beaten and has had lots of lovely lucerne etc., and I feel we should give the owner, brute tho' he is, twenty chips (rupees). The dog was put in a small room with a grille door and the boy comes and feeds it every night, but, and this is touching, it sometimes gets out (all the syces and people at the Vet. Hosp. are so terrified of it that they run from it) and goes into the yard where the loose-boxes are and sits by the horse, guarding it. Don't you think that is rather marvellous and faithful of the poor thing! Of course, it is *not* rabid — it was just doing a watch-dog act and now that it has been under observation for over ten days, the boy can take it away.

And while I am on the subject of rabid dogs, I must tell you of something that happened only yesterday. We went up to the Vet. hospital to take some meat to the yellow dog and to meet the new Vet.

A small black dog was on a lead and appeared to be shivering with fright so I went and talked to it — a sweepery-looking man had it, said it had a bone in its throat. The vet examined it and said it was rabid — said he would give it strychnine 'something'. I begged him to kill it more painlessly and we rushed home for my Browning pistol. Believe it or not, in the meantime, the owner was allowed to take his mad dog away and mingle with the teeming thousands in the Hyderabad bazaar, while he 'drank tea'. Fortunately one of the men said he knew where he had gone, which was quite half a mile away, dragging the poor animal after him as its legs would scarcely walk. When we got it back, our — or *my* to be exact — little pistol put it out of its misery — but Heaven only knows how many people it may have snapped at in the meantime.

Lola
Hyderabad

My diaphragm is a most interesting study of bruises — dark red, purple and jaundice yellow — and I feel like a pincushion. *All* because I tried to comfort a dog with a 'bone' in its throat — and it really had rabies, poor little thing, and had to be shot; a most pathetic sight. The bruises are not because the Doctor is rough, but that I bruise easily and when a handful of flesh has to be grabbed to receive the needle, a really devilish mark results! My Doctor is a Hungarian an eccentric and 'in love' with me — says so repeatedly, kissing my arms, takes an hour to boil up the syringe and needles, and just *won't* let me go. My Doctor is a woman — and G. says she's a Lesbian. That's what Hyderabad does for one. She has had two husbands, one an Afghan, and both have left her because she is too masculine, she says. She is violently jealous of anyone I speak of nicely and drives G. to distraction with her thick Hungarian English, her screams of welcome and her continual impassioned and ear-splitting voice. But she is the only Doctor in whom I have any faith at all — she *does* sterilise — she has a spotlessly clean surgery (in the bazaar where she lives in a fascinating ex-Hindu house above a line of shops) and was once in the R.A.M.C. holding the rank of a British major!

Her speciality is psycritry ... psychiatry — *goodness* — what the good old British troops called a 'trick-cyclist', if you know what I mean — and if there's anyone who needs doing over with her own medicine, it is Lola. She has an excellent brain, with none to exercise it on — says she will be put into jug if she goes back to Hungary and she can't get a passport to leave Pakistan because she was once a police suspect (so I am told by Steenie, the Policeman's wife). She wails at me that I never come and see her except when I have to (!) and that she has far more need of me than the donkeys and horses and cats I love so well — my charity should be for *her* — etc., ad lib. at the top of her corncrake voice. So we occasionally ask her to dinner with the Padre and a Missionary or — see one of my sketches to you. I am terribly sorry for her, she is a little fat dump and almost starves herself during the day to get thinner and then in the evening eats whole chickens, all done up in a greasy Hungarian fashion, at a sitting, because she is so hungry! Half an hour or so of her company and I feel like chewed string. I am completely exhausted and can't think of a word to say. I am sure she has a Vampire nature and completely drains my vitality, but she is *zo* kind 'Apreeeel — my ANNJUL' so I just put up with all this nonsense. She says she '*hates* pushing ze needle into my so Beeeautiful white skin' and wishes I would go to some Dr. who *hated* me — it would be easier. Couldn't someone put her into a book — she is a wonderful study.

The injection.

Hyderabad

As I write the Mistri is hammering and sawing and mending our wooden boxes. But the cool weather that is supposed to descend upon Hyderabad in December just hasn't materialised and it is hot — still *hot* — and I wear the same next-to-nothing clothes that I did in May and June. Am I never to feel cool? What wouldn't I give for some nice ice and snow or even a good exciting FOG!

We are due to leave this unrelenting desert on Dec. 21st and spend Christmas in Karachi in an hotel, and Geoffrey will be able once again to sing carols in his father's old church, Holy Trinity. then we get the 'Aronda' for Chittagong on Dec. 31st and shall spend New Year on the Indian Ocean. Where are my 'Quells' I wonder? There is no hope of buying any more in this country because, as I told you, all imports have been stopped for many months now. Even the most vital drugs are not procurable for the Hospitals, which is a terrible thing. Fortunately, I made a 'corner' in razor-blades some time ago, or Geoffrey wouldn't be able to shave.

And now I must stop and do the things I don't want to. This climate *never* seems to cool and today I am sitting where I have all the scorching summer — in a darkened dining-room, the windows and doors all being closed against the heat, the fan overhead and electric lights to see by. Even the verandas with the chicks down are far too hot for comfort.

A fine puggaree.

On goats and others

Quetta goats are small and befurred. Sukkur goats have tiny pointed ears — Hyderabad goats wear their ears to their knees and are as big as donkeys. Some of the sheep in Quetta have black legs and tummies and their tops creamy white.

All-white tonga-ponies everywhere are white for painting — tan legs and rocking-horse spots — purple circles or red and yellow spots are worn. Even a bull-terrier-type dog I saw at Kotri had his face and ears painted in blue and he looked very self-conscious, poor pet.

I first thought the hens balancing atop the camels among the pots and pans and babies were tied on, but now I find that they are not and that they just flutter at will among the rest of the luggage.

Bullocks in Upper Sind look like mice as they pull enormous haystacks; the cart is quite hidden and so low and small that the driver is usually just a beard and a pair of eyes behind the byl's tails.

Horses like to be hand-fed, and the owners squat at their heads putting choice handfuls of green lucerne into their mouths.

Car in the canal
Hyderabad

This is not going to be a long letter because I am busy and must give my mind to all sorts of things I'm not interested in and to write to you this morning is my bit of fun; also I must tell you of Friday's adventure. Definition of the word may be 'Discomfort seen at a distance' though my Oxford Dictionary says 'Unexpected or exciting experience'.

There are some Missionaries living way out beyond Tundo Alleyluia — forty miles of main road and then about ten along the canal bund, and there we went last Friday, taking with us a rather fat and floppy dame from here, also Missionary and the dark-skinned Padre, Emmanuel Mall — also the whole of the back of the big station-wagon full of books wrapped in huge gunny-bags, plus vegetables and meat for the Missionaries, ourselves and the Driver and my little white puppy, Blanche's child and his inseparable pal, a half-grown kitten, Little Black. They were as good as gold and sat in our very large specially-made travel basket for cats and made neither peep nor squeak. Geoffrey drove along the bund — the canal had completely overflowed itself, lapping onto the very narrow bund which was wet and slippery in parts and one had to drive very carefully. But we made it, and had lunch with what seemed dozens of talking people and children.

We tried to get away early after lunch but the floppy Missionary wanted to stay a little longer; the black Padre walked the compound surrounded by a retinue of converts drinking in his discourses, and a cup of tea was suggested — and so, of course, we didn't get away until nearly 4 o'clock. You'll see the reason for my regret in a few minutes — and may I remind you that our car is a very big Chevrolet, high off the ground and seats nine people comfortably and looks like a great sand-coloured BUS. As I am quite used to driving on some of the very narrow bits of road when we go to Karachi and G. never does and says he feels it is just like driving on a tight rope and a great strain, I thought I had better drive back — oh, dear! We did nine miles out of the ten, going slowly and me concentrating like fury, but even during the few hours that we had stayed at the bungalow, the canal had risen more — if possible. I suddenly felt my left-hand wheel being pulled as though we had a puncture and in a split-second the car was at a 45° angle axle-deep in the water and the reeds and rushes and I thought we were going to turn over — but I did pull up immediately, about a yard from a tree and we all crept out on the right-hand side like people climbing from a wreck! There wasn't a hope of moving the car ourselves and the sun was setting. Goodness! I did feel miserable.

The fat Emmanuel and our Driver rushed off in the wake of some women carrying lucerne on their heads as we thought there must be a village near but it was nearly an hour before they came back over the fields of cotton and barbul-trees in a bullock cart. G. attached our long towing-chain to the cart and he and the others pulled on the window-frames with rope in case the car heeled-over completely. The Missionary lady wasn't used to these adventures and was feeling ominous, *and* the sun went down with a bang and there wasn't a moon until midnight. The bullocky went off three rupees to the good and, with no towing done, G. and the Padre started to walk to the main road with a view to getting to Mirpur Khas for a tractor while the Missionary lady and I walked up and down trying to keep warm.

Then G. returned quite suddenly with a tall young Zemindar (farmer) carrying a rifle over his shoulder who assured us that he would call up his village and get us out in no time, and if that was impossible we should stay the night in his village and have a party! But he too then vanished into the pitch darkness.

The Zemindar was away for so long that we had to have Padre Emmanuel's assurance that he really would return and keep his word but, at last, through the cotton-fields came bobbing lanterns and I should think nearly thirty men. They first lit a huge thorn bonfire and the sparks flew up in the chilly wind and got lost among the stars. Then they cut masses of cotton-branches and some of them waded thigh-deep into the water and some pulled and others thrust the branches under the car — or tried to. But by this time the car was sinking more and was terribly heavy and they just didn't make any impression at all except to wobble it a little straighter. The huge bonfire made us warm and I began to feel better — eventually, after G. had taken out the spade we always carry, and dug little roads for the two front wheels and we had tied ropes to everything that would take it along the right side of the car, G. decided he would risk starting the engine. So, after the most strenuous efforts possible, the heavy car suddenly bounded clear onto the bund again. You may imagine the CHEERS!

And, d'you know, G. couldn't get a single man to take any reward at all — not even money to buy a sheep and have a party for themselves. After our bitter experiences with these town Sindis, we felt completely amazed to find such a wonderful spirit of help and generosity — the young Zemindar put his arms around G. and hugged him repeatedly. His name was Dost Mohammed — and G. made a pun saying he was *his* dost too, dost meaning 'friend' at which everyone laughed nicely — but even then he wouldn't let us go; he and another man came in the car until we got to the main road, just in case the banks had broken and we would have more trouble — it meant quite a long walk back for them too, wasn't it sweet of them?

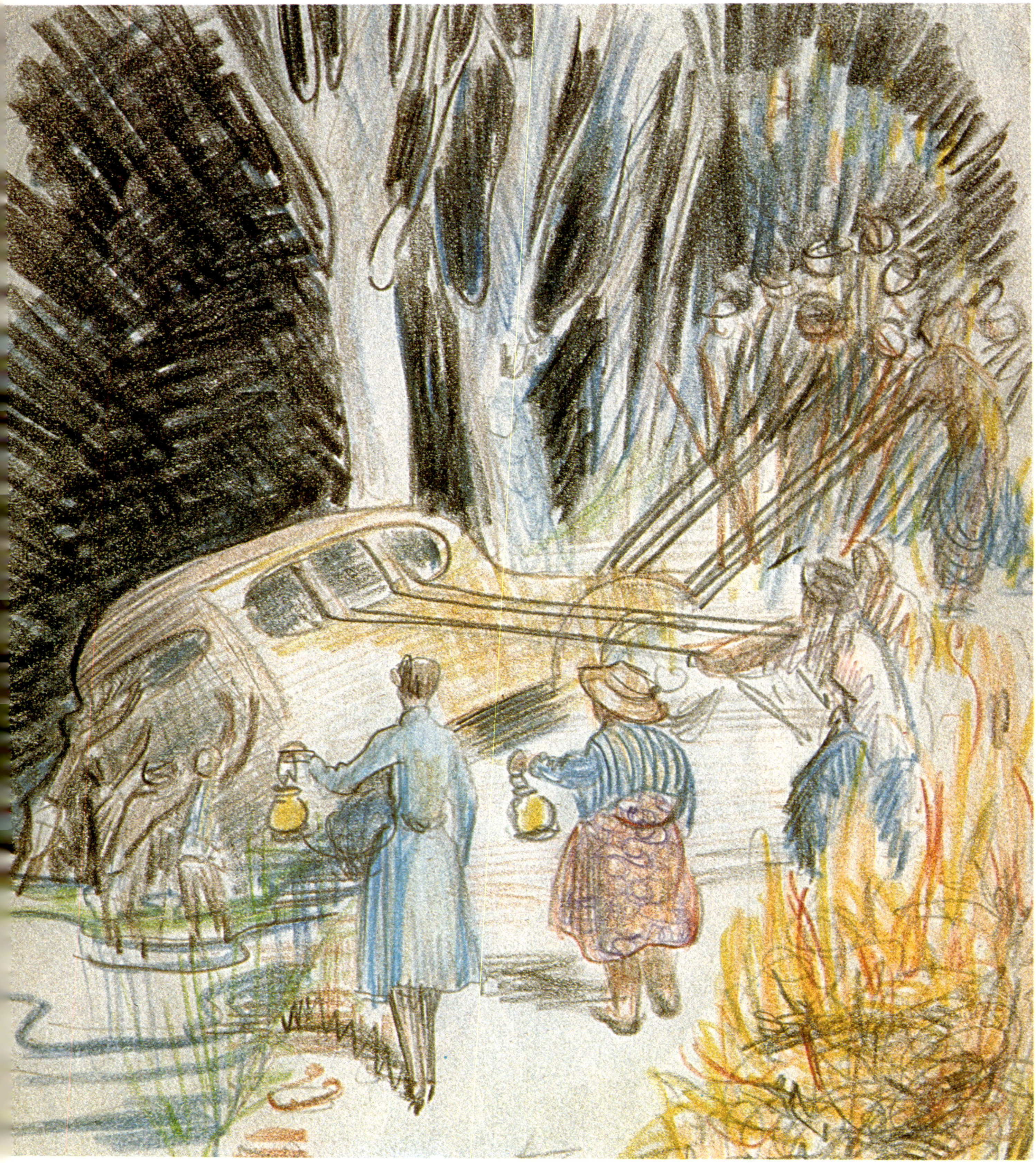

And when we said goodbye in the darkness there were yet more hugs for G. I rather wished he had hugged me too — he was a very tall and good-looking young man — but he was courteous in the Muslim fashion and didn't even look at me!

The Brothers

The Brothers have departed and the house suddenly seems quietly peaceful.

It all came about very suddenly, although we had given them provisional notice at the beginning of the month but — true to form — the Brothers had to create the maximum of disturbance, sulk, harbour resentment and behave as though they had been wronged of their birthright before departing.

Our trouble was all over G's bathwater and who should stay until the waterman put it in. G. had been in the Capital for a night and a day, and before I drove the car down to meet the 9 p.m. train, I gave orders that a hot bath must be ready. Usually, we have our baths about 7.30 p.m. but after a long journey through the hot and dusty desert, G. needed a bath directly he arrived. Suddenly, almost as though it were pre-arranged, both men looked mutinous — and so I repeated the order in a rather firmer tone — and then came the deluge of Urdu and they said they would quit next day. I realised that Sikander must have been smoking his dope again, otherwise he would never have dreamed of behaving in this way; but I am tired of pampered and lazy servants and so they are paid up next morning and told to go; and given more than excellent references — because I cannot bear to think of anyone being out of a job — and not because they deserved them.

Later, I went over to the quarter that Kullander has and said 'goodbye' to his nice smiley wife, small Crown of Mohammed and the fast-growing baby, Rose of Islam, and the old and completely toothless grandmother. I took them all presents — a blue georgette shawl for the wife; a quilt for granny to keep warm her old bones; some sweets and a bright new rupee for Taj (who, no doubt, had to hand it over to father as soon as I had gone) and tins of condensed milk for the baby, who should have been weaned and need something nice to drink — and finally, some oranges and honey, some Lyle's syrup and a bottle of lemon squash to drink in the train. We then told the driver to take them and their masses of household possessions down to the station in the big car, and we ourselves went for a walk.

So now in their stead we have two darling old things who have seen service with British sahibs all over the continent. But it is

Facing page: The car in the canal.

so long since they had Bearer's employment that one can positively see them digging down into their memories to the Good Old Days before 1947; and they both talk of the Army Sahibs they served, every one of whom seems to have a positive halo round his name. I doubt that we can live up to this glorified Past.

To bridge the gap of half a day, we had little Akbar in — and almost the first thing he did was to break a plate and a cup from a set that has remained intact for a year; and there are but three more weeks to go!

The new Bearers

November 28th, 1953

The two little old Bearers, Dildar and Abdul Rahim, work *so* hard and I have to beg them to cease their tidying and polishing and *rest!* After a while, they see that I mean it and do; but one says 'he wouldn't like any complaints'. Abdul Rahim has gone through all our drawers, putting underclothes, handkerchiefs, socks and shirts into neat piles; he has inspected the wall cupboards and wardrobes and, as evidently they do not come up to standard, he has re-hung all our clothes. I found that even my knitted woollies and fragile angora cardigan had all been carefully put on coat-hangers, the wooden ends poking and stretching them dreadfully; so I took them off and folded them back on their shelf, explaining gently, not to hurt his feelings. He said he now understood, and if I would give him some nice moth-balls, he would sprinkle the shelves with them. I again had to say 'No' — so he then gave a small smile and said 'As Mem-sahib wishes' obviously casting me to outer darkness!

Interior decoration

December 7th

My quiet blue sitting-room is quite unrecognisable, owing to Abdul Rahim's early morning zeal. The two large white rugs are laid diamondwise on the tiled floor, and on them all the chairs have been arranged in a precise circle around the small tea-table. My carved Kashmir workbox, which normally stands on its own little feet in front of the fireplace next to my sewing-chair, is now skied on top of an oblong table which is usually by the window to hold cigarette-box and ashtrays; this is now useless in a far corner; and on top of the workbox lid is a vase of flowers. Across the fireplace is a large drawing-board draped with the gaudy pink-patterned bedspread that the cats have at night to keep any draughts off their basket; and a piece of blue and white bed-ticking which I had intended for a polishing cloth is arranged in folds across the top of an armchair. It will take me days to get the room back to normal, if I am not to hurt his very sensitive feelings! Somehow, my sitting-room decor never seems to appeal to the servants — perhaps it is too casual.

The rains again

After the last sandstorm, which seemed to go on for a week, but with truth I must say it was only for four days and nights, with a temperature around 120, we are now a little cooler, 98 the best we can get to for the past three days. Just when one felt that the final misery had been reached and not another day nor another degree of heat could be borne, with the setting sun the RAIN came — in a torrential downpour which lasted for forty-eight hours. Clad in the briefest, I rush out into the darkness to the still red-hot brick chiboutra (sitting place) and let the deluge pour over me, while the thunder rumbled and the lightning played around the inky skies.

Every catastrophe under Heaven seems to have smitten Hyderabad and, with torrential rain and thunderstorms, the roads are like lakes and all the poor little mud houses fall down. All the household seems to have been ill and we have been practically servantless for a week.

G. sent a posse of men to help the poor old Dirzee who is 96 and whose sons were slaughtered by the Hindus in Agra during the civil war in 1947; he lives alone with two little grandchildren and has nobody to help him clear the deep water from his hut. What the state of the poor refugees who lived in wretched filth and squalor at the foot of the Fort can be, I dare not think. Their lot is bad enough when the weather is dry, but now that all Hyderabad is a lake and there are feet of water everywhere, it must be very terrible. Goodness! it is an unjust world.

Home

Yes — Home... HOME... that is what I keep saying to myself! And I feel that I shall just sit and make daisy-chains and smell the green grass for ever and ever. No more deserts for me!

A holy place in Hyderabad.

    I am so glad to hear of your invitation to spend the winter abroad, and you will certainly love the change and different life for a while.

    It seems to me that life is so short, and none of us ever seems to escape completely from our ghosts. But the unknown quantity just around the corner — the Future — always promises fair; so take it hopefully.

Glossary

achkan: knee-length coat
aloo: potato (here, 'Old Arloo' is the author's name for a particular potato vendor)

baksheeh: alms; a gratuity
basha: hut
bazaar: market-place
bearer: household or hotel servant
bistra: bed-roll; valise
B.O.R.: British Other Rank
bottley-wallah: pedlar of old bottles
box-wallah: employee of a business house
  derogatorily — somebody in business or commerce who is not a 'pukka-sahib'
bund: embankment, causeway, dam
bundobast: arrangement, settlement
burkha: loose garment with veiled eye-holes
burra: large
burra-din: great day; festive day
burra-sahib: master; important male European
bustee: collection of huts; small settlement
buttee: hurrican lamp
byl: bullock
bylee-wallah: driver of a small, two-wheeled vehicle drawn by two oxen

cantonment: military station and its living quarters
chapatti: thin cake of unleavened bread
chappli: sandal
char: tea
charpoy: a simple, native bedstead
chatti: water-pot
chela: disciple; pupil; servant
chiboutra: sitting-place
chick: bamboo and twine (window) screen
chiel: bird of prey
chip: a piece of money (here, a rupee)
chit or chitty: testimonial; a written note
chokidar: night-watchman; door-keeper
chota hazri: light, early breakfast
consamer: *see* khansama
coolie: labourer

cutcha: raw; unfinished (cutcha road=of earth only)

dai: midwife
dengue: a tropical fever
dhal: purée of pulse; split pulse
dhobi: washerman
dhoti: loincloth for males
dirzee: tailor
dome: lower order of untouchable who deals with corpses
dost: friend
durbar: court; levee; reception

gharry: carriage for hire
ghat: a landing place; steps by a river
godown: warehouse; storeroom
gunny-bag: bag made of coarse fabric or sacking

hamal: porter (here, a dusting-boy)
haroosh: noisy fuss; rumpus
hookah: water-cooled tobacco-pipe
howdah: seat on elephant's back
hur: armed bandit

Id: a festival or religious observance among Mohammedans

Jagganath (Juggernaut): an idol of Vishnu paraded annually at Puri in a huge vehicle; that vehicle
jarool: tree giving a substance used in making besoms
jungli (junglo): wild, unpolished man

khansama: house steward (here, cook)
khitmutgar: table-servant
kohl: powder used to darken eyelids

lota: small metal pot
lungi: man's loincloth

Maharajah: great Indian prince
Maharani: Maharajah's consort

mahout: elephant keeper and driver
Mahratta: one of a warlike Indian tribe
maidan: large open space; parade ground
mali: gardener
mamoon: maternal aunt
Marwari: man of the Jodhpur country
masjid: mosque
mem-sahib: married (European) lady
Mir: chief, leader
mistri: craftsman (here, carpenter)
moti: custodian of a mosque
mullah: Muslim teacher
Muharram: first month of Mohammedan lunar year when it is unlawful to make war; period of fasting and public mourning in memory of the death of Hassan and his brother Husain AD 669 and 680
mussac: water container made of skin
mussoola boat: surf boat

Nawab: Indian nobleman
Nawabsadah: Nawab's oldest son
nimbu pani: lemonade
nullah: ravine; water-course
numda: saddle-cloth

oont: camel

pan (pawn): betel-leaf
Pathan: inhabitant of NW Pakistan and SE Afghanistan
peon: messenger
pi-dog: common mongrel; pariah-dog
Phenyle: household disinfectant
posteen: Afghan sheepskin coat
powrah: digging implement
puggaree: light turban; hat scarf
pukka: thorough-going
pukka-sahib: gentleman
punka: ceiling fan
punt: fast trot by horses
purdah: women's apartment; exclusion of women

P.W.D.: Public Works Department

Quadi-i-Azam: great leader; Jinnah's title at independence

Rajput: descendant of original ruling and military class of Rajputana
Ramadan: great Islamic period of fasting
rickshaw: small two-wheeled carriage usually drawn by a man
R.I.N.: Royal Indian Navy

sadhu: holy man; wise man
safa: head or hat covering
sahib: honorific used in addressing Europeans; gentleman
salaam: salutation
sari: woman's principal garment
sepoy: native soldier; policeman
shalwar: loose, baggy trousers
shamiana: large tent; marquee, canopy
sirdar: commander; leader
sowar: trooper; mounted policeman or attendant
stupa: Buddhist memorial shrine
suttee: burning of widow on husband's pyre
syce: groom

talwar: curved sword
tarbush: fez
thug: robber; assassin
thuggee: the practice of thugs
tiffin: light meal; luncheon
tonga: light, two-wheeled vehicle

wadi: water-course (dry except in wet season)
wallah: person — usually a man engaged in a specific task, e.g. char-wallah; maker and vendor of tea

zemindar: land-owner; farmer
zenana: apartments in which women are secluded

*April Swayne-Thomas;
portrait by Philip Moysey.*